Apostolic Church Planting

Changing the World One Church at a Time

Steve Smith

Radical Publishing

Published by Radical Publishing

ISBN: 979-8-9960233-0-1

Endorsements

Some messages you choose to write. Others choose you. This book is the latter.

Apostolic Church Planting: Changing the World One Church at a Time by Pastor Steve Smith arises from a burden and a vision that disrupt comfort and challenge routine. It is a call that has been wrestled with and ultimately obeyed.

Seeing cities filled with people who have yet to encounter the Gospel's transformative power is unsettling. Measuring success by what we gather rather than what we send feels wrong. The same Spirit who ignited the Church in Acts is still calling, still sending, still commissioning.

This book addresses that purpose.

While burden can weigh us down, passion infuses this message with life. It is a genuine fire forged through sacrifice and faith, compelling action rather than mere words. You will feel this pull toward a calling as you read.

Vision allows us to see beyond the present into what must be. This book repositions church planting at the heart of the Apostolic mission, challenging the drift from multiplication to maintenance, from sending to settling, and from obedience to delay.

Its compelling nature lies in its honesty. It portrays church planting as costly and uncertain, yet sustained by God's faithfulness.

Ultimately, this is not just a book to be read. It is an invitation.

An invitation to recover the urgency of the mission.
An invitation to shift from addition to multiplication.
An invitation to stop waiting for perfect conditions and start responding to a present call.

And for some who hold this book in their hands, it will be something more personal:

A confirmation.
A disruption.
A sending.

Because the question has never been whether God is ready to build His Church. The question is whether we are ready to go.

Toufic Azar
Missionary to the Middle East
Assemblies of the Lord Jesus Christ

I am thankful that Steve Smith has written *Apostolic Church Planting*. If ever there was a time to re-establish New Testament mission as the central focus for the Apostolic Church, it is now. In this work, the author brings his own burning passion, his inspiring and refreshing vision, his biblical credentials rooted in Acts 2:38, and the real-life experience of years on the front lines of ministry. The result is a book that creates an overwhelming desire to plant churches. This is not a book written in ivory-tower theory. It is a book written from the mission field, where sacrifice, uncertainty, and God's faithfulness become daily realities.

His honest, heartfelt sharing will stir within you a discontentment with simply holding on to the church you lead and will ignite in you a fervor for multiplying churches. The time has come to release leaders and plant the Spirit-filled churches we so desperately need.

Stop waiting for the so-called perfect time to do what God is calling you to do. Follow the example of the early Church and be faithful to your call. If you have ever received a call from God to plant a church, find some quiet time for Steve Smith's practical and timely book, *Apostolic Church Planting*. Every Apostolic leader and pastor ought to own and read this book.

Chad Erickson
Church Growth Coordinator, Missions America
Assemblies of the Lord Jesus Christ

I planted a church in 2015. This is the book I needed then. Honest, practical, and rooted in real experience, Pastor Steve Smith gives planters the conversation most of us had to figure out along the way. Reading Apostolic Church Planting felt like sitting across the table from someone who had been there before. Pastor Smith writes with conviction and the kind of hard-earned wisdom that only comes from someone who has actually done the work. He doesn't pretend to have every answer, but he hands you what most of us had to learn the hard way. If you're standing where I once stood — called, burdened, and wondering where to begin — start here. It will save you from pitfalls, and it just might launch the adventure of a lifetime."

Brandon Frazier
Pastor, Bethlehem Church
Starkville, MS

Apostolic Church Planting brings a refreshing clarity that will serve the Apostolic movement for years to come. Having met Pastor Steve Smith in person, his calm and steady demeanor is immediately evident, and that same tone carries through his writing. It's inviting, engaging, and pulls you directly into the conversation. He unpacks Kingdom principles in a way that feels both personal and powerful. Each story places you right in the middle of the mission, allowing you to experience the urgency and significance of the moment. This is far more than a collection of stories about church planting. It's a bold, awakening call to the mission God has placed before us. Read it, but be prepared. You won't walk away unchanged.

Timothy Gill
Indiana District Superintendent
Assemblies of the Lord Jesus Christ

Apostolic Church Planting is part memoir, part manifesto, and part altar call for the Apostolic movement. Pastor Steve Smith reminds us that church planting is not a side project—it is central to our mission, and the harvest is waiting for our YES.

Evan Grizzle
Assistant Director, Missions America
Assemblies of the Lord Jesus Christ

In a day and age when it's far easier to maintain than to multiply, this book is a much-needed reminder that a life of purpose begins the moment we say yes to the call of God on our lives. Pastor Smith addresses the two major obstacles of time and territory with no wasted words. You can feel the burden and hard-earned experience of my friend Pastor Steve Smith pouring out onto every page as you take this journey. By the time you finish reading, you will not only have clarity on the call, but also the confidence to act.

Zach Hammond
President, Student Ministries
Assemblies of the Lord Jesus Christ

For nearly 30 years, I have had the privilege of watching my dear friend, Steve Smith, live the message he shares in this book. *Apostolic Church Planting* is not simply a guide to church-planting strategy, it is a heartfelt call to obedience, faith, and Kingdom vision. Steve writes with conviction, humility, and real-world experience that will inspire pastors, leaders, and church planters to boldly answer God's call to reach communities with the gospel.

Bill Hobson
Former General Secretary of North American Missions
United Pentecostal Church, International

Apostolic Church Planting by Rev. Steve Smith is a timely and necessary voice calling the Church back to its Apostolic roots. This book does more than inspire. It challenges, clarifies, and compels action. With honesty, conviction, and real-world experience, Smith reminds us that church planting is not a strategy but a mandate. If we are serious about reaching our world, we must be serious about sending. This is a must-read for pastors, leaders, and anyone who feels the stirring of God to build beyond what currently exists. Brother Smith has given us the perfect mix of inspiration and instruction. With stories from the front lines and statistical insight, this book offers a perspective that can only be given by a lifetime of experience and the weight of a burden.

Cody Mayo
Pastor, The Pentecostal Church of Aimwell
Aimwell, Louisiana

Pastor Steve Smith captivates the reader—myself included—from the introduction and, with surgical precision, leads the willing on a journey of transparency that highlights the real-life challenges of church planting. Having spent the better part of twenty-four years of ministry, devoting my strength to establish three churches, I found myself reliving personal moments and familiar battles through the pages of *Apostolic Church Planting*.

It is with my highest recommendation that I say: if kingdom advancement, revival, and reaching lost humanity truly matter within your calling, then pick up this book and voraciously absorb the practical and eternity-impacting truths it contains.

Every apostolic minister would do well to read this testimony of Heaven's purpose lived out. A wayward world is still waiting to be reached, and this book is a timely reminder that true anointing is always revealed on the other side of personal sacrifice.

Robert Mitchell
Bishop, Vertical Church
Centennial, Colorado

Steve Smith is at heart an Apostolic church planter with unwavering passion. I had the privilege of witnessing his church plant in New York up close, and his friendship and example helped shape my ministry as a young pastor. May this book serve as an impartation of Apostolic principles and passion to another generation.

Jonathan Sanders
Pastor, Pentecostal Tabernacle
Kerman, California

Apostolic Church Planting, written by Pastor Steve Smith, is a vital and timely resource for the Apostolic movement. Pastor Smith offers a wealth of insight drawn directly from his experience in the field, coupled with his deep dedication to being a student of the Word. His relentless hunger to learn and grow as a man, a pastor, and a leader shines through on every page.

Reading this book inspired me personally to become more intentional about sending church planters. It challenged me to better support those who have taken the plunge to start new works in the communities where God has called them.

One of my favorite moments in the manuscript is found in Chapter 8. Pastor Steve shares a story about a pastor who, after an exhausting day of work and ministry, found himself staring down a foot-long chili cheese dog from Sonic. The question hit him: "Can God bless a chili cheese dog?" It is these kinds of relatable stories and honest reflections that keep you turning pages. By the final chapter, you do not just feel informed. You feel compelled and commissioned. The end of the book is not the end of the story. It is a Great Commissioning to go out and bring souls home.

Thank you, Pastor Steve, for using your gifts to enlarge the Kingdom and inspire us all with *Apostolic Church Planting*.

Joshua Wilson
General Secretary
Assemblies of the Lord Jesus Christ

What you are reading is testimony and not just theory. Steve Smith writes from the trenches, having put his own hands to the plow and his heart into the harvest. You can feel it in every page: a burden for souls, a love for the Kingdom, and a clear understanding that this work is about eternal matters, not temporary gain.

With a heritage shaped by a father who promoted Sunday School and valued reaching people, that same passion now flows through his own ministry.

More than a book, it's a burden put into words, a reminder that the work is urgent, and a call to action to reach the lost.

Steve Wilson
Former General Superintendent
Assemblies of the Lord Jesus Christ

Dedication

To my wife, Lorrie, your faith, strength, and unwavering support have made this journey possible. Thank you for standing beside me in every season and for believing in the call of God on our lives.

To our sons, Landry, Clancy, and Colyer, you are my greatest joy and my greatest responsibility. My prayer is that you will each hear the voice of God, follow His calling, and do something great for His Kingdom.

Contents

Foreword

It is with a full heart and a deep sense of Kingdom responsibility that I commend this work by Pastor Steve Smith to the body of Christ. In a generation rich with opportunity yet often distracted by lesser pursuits, *Apostolic Church Planting* calls us back to the sacred center of our Apostolic identity—the burden for souls and the divine mandate to go.

From the opening pages, it is clear that this book is not written from a distance but from the altar of experience. It carries the tone of a shepherd, the conviction of a preacher, and the weight of one who has walked through seasons of calling, sacrifice, uncertainty, and divine confirmation. Pastor Smith does not present theory; he presents testimony. And there is something about lived truth that speaks with a clarity that cannot be manufactured.

As a fellowship, the Assemblies of the Lord Jesus Christ has always stood firmly upon the unchanging message of Acts 2:38. That message is not simply something we defend—it is something we must declare. It was never meant to remain within the walls of established congregations. It was born in revival, carried by movement, and sustained through multiplication. Church planting, therefore, is not an optional ministry emphasis. It is the very expression of Apostolic obedience.

This book reminds us that the Church was never designed to settle. It was designed to send.

What I appreciate most about this work is its honesty and its balance. It does not glamorize the journey. It speaks plainly of the cost, the questions, and the moments when faith must stand even when clarity is limited. Yet woven through every chapter is the steady and unshakable testimony that God is faithful. The same Spirit who moved in the Book of Acts is still calling, still sending, and still building His Church today.

There is a pastoral weight in these pages that I believe will speak deeply to every reader. To pastors, it offers a gentle but firm challenge to move beyond addition and embrace multiplication. To church planters, it offers strength and reassurance that calling will sustain what enthusiasm cannot. To leaders who feel a stirring but seek confirmation, it provides both clarity and counsel. And to the local church, it presents a higher vision—not merely to grow, but to become a sending force in the Kingdom of God.

As I reflect on the message of this book, I am reminded that true Apostolic ministry is never territorial. It is always missional. We are not called to protect what we have built but to participate in what God is building. The Kingdom does not advance through preservation alone. It advances through propagation. It advances when men and women hear the voice of God and respond with a willing yes.

There is a question that quietly yet powerfully rises from these pages: Are we ready to respond?

In my years of ministry, I have observed that the greatest moves of God have never been the result of perfect conditions. They have always been the result of yielded lives. When individuals and churches align themselves with the purpose of God, Heaven responds. And when Heaven responds, cities are changed, families are restored, and truth is established where darkness once prevailed.

I believe this book arrives not by accident but by divine timing. The harvest is great. The need is urgent. The Spirit is still speaking. And the call is still going forth.

My prayer is that as you read, you will not only be informed—you will be stirred. That something deep within your spirit will be awakened. That hesitation will give way to faith, and that faith will give way to action.

Pastor Smith has not merely written a book. He has extended a call.
May we hear it.
May we embrace it.
And by the grace of God, may we answer it.

Kenneth Carpenter
General Superintendent
Assemblies of the Lord Jesus Christ

Introduction

Well, hello.

I'm genuinely glad we get to sit down together for this conversation. I've wanted to talk about Apostolic church planting for a long time, not because I consider myself an expert. I don't. Most of us in the Apostolic movement aren't "experts" in church planting. Most church planters start one church. Some start two. That experience doesn't make us gurus.

But it does give us stories.

And stories matter. When Apostolic men and women gather and tell their church-planting stories, the victories, the mistakes, the miracles, the awkward first services, the financial scares, the unexpected breakthroughs, something powerful happens. Patterns begin to surface. Principles rise to the top. Hard-earned lessons become shared wisdom. That's not a small thing. That's the Church learning to build together.

The fact that you picked up this book already tells me something about you. You likely identify as Apostolic. You believe Acts 2:38 still declares the biblical plan of salvation. You are convinced that repentance, water baptism by immersion in the Name of Jesus Christ, and the infilling of the Holy Ghost with the initial evidence of speaking in other tongues as the Spirit gives utterance form the New Testament response to the gospel. That conviction isn't a footnote to your faith. It's the foundation.

If that's not your story, you're still welcome here. Truly. I'm glad you're reading. Just understand that I'll frame this conversation around planting churches that boldly preach and consistently practice the Apostolic message. That is the lens through which these pages are written.

I'm also not writing to one organization. I'm not assuming you belong to a particular fellowship or that you belong to one at all. I believe far more unites modern Apostolics than divides us. We share a message. We share a burden. We share a calling to reach our world. That common ground is the table where this conversation takes place.

Let me say something up front: I reserve the right to grow.

If you disagree with something in these pages, there's a good chance I may refine, expand, or even revise my thinking in the years ahead. I want to be that kind of leader and that kind of writer. Certainty without humility is a dangerous thing, especially in Kingdom work. So I hold these ideas with conviction and with open hands.

This book doesn't attempt to answer every conceivable question about church planting. That would be an impossible task. Instead, I want to invite you into an honest, transparent, and deeply practical conversation about something that matters eternally to the Kingdom of God.

Church planting is not a side project.

It is not a trend we follow when ministry feels stale. It is not a strategy we experiment with when everything else has failed. Church planting is central to Apostolic mission, and it has been since the Book of Acts. The Early Church didn't wait for the culture to become favorable. They didn't wait for comfortable facilities or polished programs. They planted. They preached. They trusted the Holy Ghost to do what only He can do.

And He showed up.

That same Spirit who moved in Jerusalem, Judea, Samaria, and the uttermost parts of the earth is still moving today. He is still calling people. He is still anointing planters. He is still confirming the Word with signs following. The question is not whether God is ready to build His Church. The question is whether we are ready to be used in that building.

This won't read like a textbook. If that's what you're looking for, you may find this a little too personal, a little too raw. These pages will feel more like a long, unhurried conversation across a table. I'll share principles not because I invented them, but because I've watched them work. I'll share stories not to impress you, but to connect with you. I'll tell you what worked, what didn't, and what I'm still learning.

The planters who have planted multiple churches? We especially need to listen to them.

Their scars and their successes carry a kind of weight that classrooms can't replicate. When they speak, lean in. There is gold in their experience.

This book is my best attempt to gather some of that gold and put it in your hands.

So, fix your favorite drink. Settle into your favorite chair.

Let's talk about building churches that change communities, cities, and nations. Let's talk about the kind of planting that doesn't just add another address to a city map but shifts the spiritual atmosphere of a place. Let's talk about what it looks like to trust God radically, lead wisely, and build something that outlasts us.

The conversation you've been waiting to have? It starts right here.

Part 1: The Calling

"*Before I formed thee in the belly I knew thee; and before thou camest forth out of the womb I sanctified thee, and I ordained thee a prophet unto the nations*" (Jeremiah 1:5).

"*The place God calls you to is the place where your deep gladness and the world's deep hunger meet.*" - Frederick Buechner

Chapter One

The Adventure of a Lifetime

I will never forget the moment I stared at a little plastic stick in my wife's hand. A simple home pregnancy test. That flimsy device, bought for a few dollars at a neighborhood drugstore, stood ready to announce the direction of our destiny.

One line meant life would continue as usual. Two lines meant bottles, diapers, late-night burping sessions, and a brand-new identity were waiting around the corner.

We stood there in silence and watched.

Like a mirage shimmering above a West Texas highway, that second line slowly appeared. Faint at first, then darker, then unmistakable.

Two lines.

Decorate the nursery. Pick a name. Call the grandparents. Life will never be the same.

That was the year 2000. Since then, God has blessed us with three children who transformed our home into a laboratory of laughter, chaos, prayer, forgiveness, growth, and joy. Not every day has been easy. Some days tested every ounce of patience and faith we possessed. But not one day has been mundane. Parenthood stretched us, sanctified us, and strengthened us.

Around that same time, God unfolded another adventure, one that demanded as much faith, sacrifice, and endurance as parenthood itself. A few months before our first child was born, my wife and I stood before our home church in West Memphis, Arkansas. Our pastor, Bobby McCool Jr., announced that God was calling us to plant a church in the New York City metro area.

Two lines had already changed our family. Now two words changed our future: New York.

That night God confirmed the call through tongues and interpretation: "I was there in your calling, and I will be there in your destination."

That promise anchored our souls. It steadied us through financial strain, sleepless nights, cultural adjustments, and moments of utter uncertainty. God finishes what He starts, even when our strength runs thin. Paul expressed that confidence: "He which hath begun a good work in you will perform it until the day of Jesus Christ" (Philippians 1:6).

Looking back, I see something important. God birthed two things in us at the same time. He birthed children in our home and a burden in our spirit. He grew our family and our faith simultaneously. In many ways, church planting feels a lot like that pregnancy test moment. You wait. You pray. You hope. And then, two lines appear.

Life will never be the same.

Birthing Churches, Birthing Children

Birthing a church feels a lot like birthing a child. There is pain. There is sacrifice. There are tears. But there is also indescribable joy.

When you hold a newborn baby for the first time, you understand you are participating in something divine. You did not just produce life. You steward it. You sense eternity in your hands. Church planting carries that same sacred weight. You pray over empty rooms before anyone else sees potential. You preach to small crowds when momentum feels microscopic. You lie awake at night wondering if you misheard God.

Then one day, you celebrate a first baptism with tears streaming down your face. You watch marriages heal. You watch addicts walk free. You watch children lift their hands in worship for the first time.

And something inside you whispers, *This is eternal.*

Most church planters I know would not trade the experience for anything. They live the adventure of a lifetime. They stand on the front lines of God's redemptive work. They watch the gospel change families and the Spirit restore what sin once destroyed.

Missionary James Gribble captured the spirit of a pioneer: "I shall be content with the lowest seat in heaven, if only there I may sit and see the redeemed of the Lord come in from those fields where I have been a pioneer missionary." That statement defines the heartbeat of a church planter.

Children do not arrive fully grown, and neither do churches. Babies begin small, fragile, and full of potential. So do church plants. In the early days, a planter may carry more hope than visible results. Attendance may be small. Finances may be tight. But that does not mean nothing significant is happening.

It simply means life is still developing.

Many leaders are tempted to despise small beginnings. Yet God is comfortable starting small. Jesus compared the kingdom of God to a mustard seed, something tiny enough to overlook, yet powerful enough to grow into something that blesses its entire environment (Matthew 13:31–32). A church plant may begin in a living room or a school cafeteria. But if God is in it, "small" does not mean "insignificant."

Church planting is not merely work. It is stewardship. It is faith with skin on it.

The True Strength of a Church

We often measure churches by seating capacity. Heaven measures them by sending capacity.

The world does not need more impressive buildings or polished productions. It needs more gospel-preaching, Spirit-filled churches planted where the hope of Jesus remains distant or unknown.[1] If we want to change a city's culture, plant a church. If we want to shape the next generation, plant a church.

So instead of merely bemoaning politics, plant churches. Instead of fretting about the economy, plant churches. Instead of wringing our hands over society's moral direction, plant churches.

Jesus declared, "Upon this rock I will build my church; and the gates of hell shall not prevail against it" (Matthew 16:18). He purchased the church with His own blood (Acts 20:28). When church planters step into an unevangelized or under-evangelized community, they do not go alone. Calvary paid the bill. Heaven backs the mission. The presence of God goes with them.

Church planting stands at the very heart of the Great Commission: go, teach, baptize, teach again. And Jesus added this promise: "I am with you always, even unto the end of the world" (Matthew 28:20).

That promise still holds.

Breaking Through Time and Territory

If all of this rings true, then an honest question demands an answer. Why do we not plant more churches? Over the years, I have sat across tables from dozens of church planters. Almost every conversation circles back to the same two obstacles that slow multiplication.

They are rarely theological problems. They are almost always practical ones: time and territory.

The Obstacle of Time

I once read about a study in which churches of various sizes were asked, "Do you want to start a daughter work?" Almost all responded, "Yes." Then they were asked, "When?" The overwhelming answer was, "When we're a little bigger."[2]

That response reveals something about human nature. We love the idea of multiplication, eventually. We applaud it in theory. We celebrate it from a distance. But when the moment arrives to release leaders, families, and resources into a new work, hesitation creeps in.

We admire multiplication until it costs us something, but you simply cannot out-give God.

An old story illustrates this well. A man asked his friend, "If you had one hundred bales of hay, would you give me fifty?" His friend replied, "Of course." "If you had ten cows, would you give me five?" "Absolutely." "If you had two hogs, would you give me one?"

The friend paused. "Man, you know I've got two hogs."

We pledge what we do not possess but protect what we already hold.

Yet here is the truth: the only essential ingredient for a church plant is a church planter. No mother, no baby. No church planter, no church plant. If God has called and equipped someone, the time is right to begin, regardless of whether the sending congregation feels large enough or comfortable enough.

That does not mean wisdom is unnecessary or planning unimportant. It simply means obedience cannot be postponed forever in the name of better circumstances.

At some point, someone has to go.

Church planters must know they are called. Every successful church planter I know carries a deep conviction that God is planting the church and they are simply the blessed instruments He has chosen to use.[3]

Calling sustains what enthusiasm cannot. Excitement is a spark. Calling is a furnace.

Emotion fades. Attendance fluctuates. Criticism comes. Bills pile up. But calling anchors the soul. When criticism comes, calling steadies you. When the bills mount, calling strengthens you. When you question your own adequacy, calling reminds you that God does not call the qualified. He qualifies the called.

The Obstacle of Territory

Pentecostals can become territorial without even realizing it. We imagine that if someone plants a church too close to ours, our congregation will shrink. We think in terms of competition instead of commission. We guard turf instead of growing the Kingdom.

But that thinking is both unbiblical and untrue.

Jesus said, "Give, and it shall be given unto you; good measure, pressed down, and shaken together, and running over" (Luke 6:38). That principle reaches far beyond finances. When we release someone with an open hand, God often sends not only more people but the exact people we need for the next season.

Gamaliel understood this in Acts 5. He warned the council not to fight a work that might actually be of God. If it were not of God, it would come to nothing. But if it was of God, they would find themselves fighting against God Himself (Acts 5:38–39).

I refuse to spend my life fighting something that just might be God's idea.

Leading with an Open Hand

A friend once attended a large Apostolic church with two gifted assistant pastors. He asked the senior pastor, "Aren't you worried one of them might split your church?" The pastor responded calmly, "I will never have a church split." My friend pressed him. "How can you be so sure?" He replied, "If one of those men rises up and starts a church, I will rush to endorse it. Just maybe, this is of God, and I missed it."

May his tribe increase.

That answer reveals the difference between protecting a personal kingdom and advancing the Kingdom of God. We do not grow the Kingdom by clenching our fists. We grow it by leading with open hands, letting God take what He wants and give what He wants in return.

And He always gives more than He takes.

I once heard of a congregation that released about twenty people, faithful saints, committed families, and two gifted leaders, to plant a church just thirty minutes away. They gave up musicians, volunteers, givers, and leaders. They chose multiplication over maintenance.[4]

Within five years, that new church supported its pastor full-time. Souls were being saved. A new lighthouse was shining. But here is the rest of the story: the very next year after the plant launched, the mother church grew by one-third.

One-third. They sent out twenty. God sent back increase. They released leaders. God raised up new ones. They opened their hands. God filled them again.

You cannot out-give God.

When Territory Turns Toxic

Not every story feels triumphant at first. I once sat in a Raising Cane's restaurant listening to a young church planter pour out their heart. God was blessing their new congregation, yet neighboring pastors were working overtime to discourage and hinder the work. It felt like a modern-day Sanballat and Tobiah opposing Nehemiah.

This young planter possessed integrity and character. He faced resistance simply because he dared to obey God. When he finished, I leaned back and asked, "Do you want to be the bishop of this city someday?" He looked confused. I told him, "You will weather this storm because your spirit is right." Joel Urshan once said, "Time will always prove you right if your attitude doesn't prove you wrong."

But my question concerned the future. When criticism passes, and your influence grows, how will you treat the next church planter who arrives? Will you perpetuate the dysfunction? Or will you champion the cause?

At the end of the day, we all claim to be Kingdom-minded. The real question is: Whose kingdom are we minding?

Business leaders understand something the church occasionally forgets. In Manhattan's Diamond District, jewelers stand shoulder to shoulder. In Memphis, car dealerships cluster along the same highway. Restaurants gather in every major city's dining district. This is not an accident. It is strategy. Proximity creates momentum. Research consistently shows that businesses operating in clusters outperform those in isolation because they generate more demand together than any single business could alone. The market grows. Customers know where to go. Everyone benefits.

What if the Apostolic church embraced that mindset? What if we linked arms instead of guarding turf?

If you believe God's resources are limited, you will guard territory. If you believe God's resources are infinite, you will celebrate multiplication. Imagine a "Dollar General spirit" sweeping across our movement, planting churches everywhere a God-called planter is willing to go. Not just strategic cities. Everywhere.

Because the harvest is far larger than we often imagine.

The Harvest Is Ready

An Apostolic statesman once suggested that a pastor could only effectively shepherd about 10,000 people, implying that we need roughly one Apostolic church for every 10,000 people.

In early 2026, the population of the United States stood at approximately 347 million. Following that model, we would need about 34,700 Apostolic churches to reach the nation.

The three largest Oneness Apostolic organizations combined total approximately six thousand churches across the United States and Canada.[5]

That leaves a gap of more than twenty-eight thousand churches.

No wonder Jesus said, "The harvest truly is plenteous, but the labourers are few" (Matthew 9:37). Can it be done? The Book of Acts offers a remarkable example. During Paul's ministry in Ephesus, within two years "all they which dwelt in Asia heard the word of the Lord Jesus" (Acts 19:10). Conservative estimates suggest that this Roman province contained five to six million people.

If God could saturate millions through Spirit-empowered believers then, He can certainly do it again.[6]

We cannot manufacture callings. Only God calls. But we can obey the command Jesus gave: "Pray ye therefore the Lord of the harvest, that he will send forth labourers into his harvest" (Matthew 9:38). The Greek word translated "send forth" is *ekballō*, the same word used to cast out demons. Jesus was not asking for polite prayers for volunteers. He was telling them to pray that God would forcefully launch workers into the harvest.

He did not tell His followers to pray primarily for resources, buildings, or even harvest. He told them to pray for laborers. When Jesus gives a prayer request, we would be wise to take it seriously.

And I have it on good authority that if we pray His prayer request, He will answer it.

A Prayer on a Bridge

Veteran missionary Alan Demos once told me something that stopped me in my tracks. He said, "God sent you to Westchester County, New York, because I asked Him to."

Years earlier, a family member living in Tarrytown, New York, had drifted from God. One night while driving across the Tappan Zee Bridge, he began to pray. Not casually. Not mechanically. He interceded. As the Hudson River stretched beneath him, he asked God to establish an Apostolic church in that region.

And heaven listened.

Years later, my family found ourselves living in Westchester County, planting a church minutes from that bridge.

Long before I sensed a call. Long before we packed a moving truck. Long before a sermon was preached, Someone had already been praying. Our church plant was not only the result of a calling. It was the result of intercession.

The story reaches even farther back. Decades earlier, in the early 1950s, his mother had prayed over Nassau County on Long Island. Several years later, D. D. Davis moved from Texas to Long Island and established Bethel United Pentecostal Church. A mother prayed. A missionary relocated. A church was planted.

Prayer preceded movement. Intercession prepared territory. Heaven answered what someone dared to ask. God still responds to bridge prayers. God still responds to midnight intercession. God still responds when someone stands in the gap for a city.

The real question is not whether God is willing to send laborers. The real question is whether we are willing to ask.

What unevangelized community is waiting on your prayer? What county has no Apostolic witness? What neighborhood needs someone to cross a bridge and plead for it? Because somewhere tonight, a church planter may be packing boxes, unaware that their calling is the answer to someone else's prayer.

Is There Not a Cause?

When David arrived at the battlefield and heard Goliath mocking Israel, his older brother rebuked him for even being there. David responded with a question that echoes across the centuries: "Is there not a cause?" (1 Samuel 17:29).

That question should become our rallying cry.

When territorialism surfaces, is there not a cause? When fear delays obedience, is there not a cause? When resources seem scarce, is there not a cause? The territory before us is vast. The time is short. The stakes are eternal.

So let us dream bigger. Let us plant more churches. Let us refuse to settle for maintenance when God has called us to multiplication. Let us live the adventure of a lifetime, the adventure of Apostolic church planting.

Nothing changes a city, a nation, or a generation quite like the planting of a truly Apostolic church.

Perhaps this chapter must end not with information, but with invitation. Somewhere God may be stirring someone's heart. Somewhere a pastor may be realizing that the answer to their city's future is not to hold on tighter, but to open their hand wider. Somewhere a young couple may be standing before their own "two lines" moment.

If that is you, do not ignore the stirring. Do not dismiss the burden. Do not postpone obedience until conditions seem safer. Choose faith. Choose generosity. Choose multiplication. Choose the Kingdom.

Because the adventure of a lifetime may begin with something as small as two lines on a test. Or two words spoken in a sanctuary. Or one prayer whispered on a bridge. And when God begins writing that story, life will never be the same.

Every church that exists today began with someone who heard the call of God and said yes.

Discussion & Application

Use these questions for personal reflection or group discussion.

1. The chapter compares church planting to a pregnancy test, a moment that divides life into before and after. What "two lines" moment has God used to redirect the trajectory of your life or ministry? How did you respond to the fear and excitement of that call?

2. The author argues that the only essential ingredient for a church plant is a church planter, yet most churches delay multiplication until they feel "big enough." What specific fears or assumptions drive that delay in your context, and how does the principle of calling challenge those assumptions?

3. Consider the congregation that released twenty people to plant a church thirty minutes away and then grew by one-third the following year. What would it take for your leadership team to move from a maintenance mindset to a multiplication mindset? What is the first practical step?

4. The chapter describes a young church planter facing resistance from neighboring pastors for obeying God. How would you counsel a planter in that situation? More importantly, how would you ensure that you do not become the obstacle when a new planter arrives in your city?

5. Alan Demos prayed on a bridge, and years later, that prayer became a church plant. Who is praying for the unevangelized communities in your region? What would it look like for your church to adopt a sustained prayer strategy for church planting in specific cities, counties, or neighborhoods?

Chapter Two

When a City Gets in Your Spirit

My wife and I sat on a darkened airplane flying home to Memphis after a spontaneous vacation through New England. We had spent a week exploring Boston, Cape Cod, and the surrounding region. It had been a much-needed getaway. Ministry had been demanding, and we had uncharacteristically not planned a real vacation that year. Then, only a few weeks before, we found a cheap flight and decided to go somewhere, anywhere, just to catch our breath.

What we thought would be a simple trip turned into something much more significant.

As our flight carried us home, I looked out the window into the night sky and saw the New York City metro horizon glowing beneath us. Millions of lights stretched in every direction. It was both breathtaking and sobering. I sat there staring at those lights, thinking about the sheer number of people represented below, and suddenly I felt overwhelmed.

I stared longer than I expected to. Because every light represented a person. And every person represented a soul. Suddenly, a thought gripped me with overwhelming force.

So many people. So few Apostolic churches.

The realization hit me deeply. We had served in a local church for more than ten years, first as youth pastor and then as associate pastor. We loved our church. We loved our pastor. We were grateful for every opportunity God had given us. But as I looked at that city, a burden began to rise in my spirit that I could not ignore.

My wife noticed my response and asked, "Are you crying?" Now, I do not cry easily. But something about that moment reached down into me in a way I had not expected. I answered her honestly: "Well, you would have to be a heathen to know that there are so many people in the New York City metro and so few Apostolic churches and not be moved."

It was not polished language. But it was the truth. In that moment, my heart was stirred by the need of that region. We both sensed we should not treat the moment casually. We agreed on the next step: when we got home, I needed to talk to our pastor, Bobby McCool Jr., and seek his counsel.

That decision matters more than some people realize.

Real calling does not make you rebellious. It drives you toward prayer, humility, and spiritual authority.

Seeking Counsel Before Taking Steps

A few days later, I sat down with Pastor McCool and told him what had happened on that plane. I described the burden I felt and the sense that God might be stirring us toward something new. He listened carefully and then gave me an answer that was both practical and prophetic.

He said this might just be God, but that neither of us knew anybody in the New York City metro area. So if this was really going to happen, it would have to be a God thing. That statement stayed with me because it was both realistic and hopeful. He was not dismissing the burden, but he was not allowing emotion to outrun wisdom either.

Over the next few weeks, I told exactly one friend about my budding interest in planting a church in the New York City metro area. I was not trying to rally support or build momentum around an idea. I was simply being honest about what God seemed to be doing in my heart.

Not long after, I was scheduled to tag-team preach at a youth rally in Wisconsin with Harold Linder from New York, a man I had only met once before. We sat down for lunch to plan the service. But instead of spending most of our time discussing the rally, I discovered that my "one friend" had already mentioned my interest in New York.

The conversation shifted immediately.

He did something deeply generous. He suggested that my wife and I fly to New York. He offered to let us stay at his home and even use his car so we could explore the metro area on our own. That was no small thing. We took him up on the offer.

And that trip changed us.

For one exhilarating week, we explored the area. We prayed. We drove. We looked. We listened. We paid attention to what stirred in our spirits. One area in particular captured our attention: Westchester County. I also had the privilege of preaching on Long Island, in Manhattan, and in Yonkers. Every step of the journey deepened rather than diminished the burden.

By the time we came home, we felt something difficult to explain but impossible to deny. We felt like we had been born in the wrong part of the world. That may sound dramatic, but it is truly how it felt. The city had gotten into our spirit. What had started as a moment on an airplane had become something more enduring.

It was no longer just an emotional response. It was beginning to feel like a calling.

Still, we did not rush ahead recklessly. Upon our pastor's recommendation, I met with our friend Jimmy Lumpkin, who had started a church in Orange, New Jersey. We also met with the Arkansas District Board, the New York Metro District Board, and the Home Missions Administrative Committee. Throughout that process, our posture was consistent. We were not trying to force our way into anything. We were seeking the direction and counsel of trusted leaders.

Genuine calling does not develop in isolation.

The Biblical Pattern of Calling

Our call to plant an Apostolic church in Westchester County was progressive. It unfolded step by step through burden, prayer, counsel, confirmation, and opportunity. And when you study Scripture, you see that this is often how God works. Sometimes He moves suddenly and dramatically. But more often, He unfolds His purpose over time, confirming it through people, circumstances, and seasons of testing.

Throughout Scripture, the expansion of God's kingdom always begins with a call. Before there was a nation, God called Abraham. Before there was deliverance, God called Moses. Before there was prophetic renewal, God called Samuel. Before there was an Apostolic church, Jesus called fishermen.[1]

Every time God wanted to extend His kingdom, He called someone to go where they had never gone before.

Genesis 12:1 records God saying to Abram, "Get thee out of thy country, and from thy kindred, and from thy father's house, unto a land that I will shew thee." God was not making a suggestion. He was issuing a summons. And notice something important: God did not show Abraham the full map before He called him to go.

That is still how calling often works.

We prefer clarity before obedience. We want details before movement. We want explanations before surrender. But God often gives just enough light for the next step and then waits to see whether we trust Him.

Signing a Blank Contract

I once heard a story about a man who vowed never to become a preacher. His father had been a preacher, and the family had always struggled financially. So he decided early that ministry was not for him. Then he fell in love with a young woman who believed God had told her she would marry a preacher.

That created quite a dilemma.

The man later said the Lord gave him a vision of a blank contract. At the bottom of the page was a line for his signature, but the page itself was empty. He objected, saying he could not sign something when he did not know what he was agreeing to. Then he sensed the Lord respond: "What does it matter? It's not what you're signing up for. It's who you're signing up for."

When God calls, it's not what you're signing up for. It's who you're signing up for.

That is often what calling feels like. It feels like signing a blank contract with God. It feels like saying yes before you know every detail of the journey. Abraham understood that. He left comfort, structure, and stability because God told him to go. Church planters understand that tension well. God often calls people away from predictable systems and comfortable environments into assignments that require deeper trust.

Burden Versus Calling

A burden and a calling can feel very similar at first. Both stir the heart. Both produce deep concern. Both can keep you awake at night. But they are not the same thing.

A burden is often seasonal. A calling is enduring. Enthusiasm cannot carry you through; calling can.

A burden is what you feel when God allows you to experience the weight of a need. It may move you to act in a moment or respond in a specific season. But a calling remains long after the initial emotion fades. It persists through difficulty, uncertainty, criticism, delay, and sacrifice.

Jesus illustrated something like this in Luke 10:33–34 with the story of the Good Samaritan. The Samaritan saw a wounded man, had compassion, and responded immediately. He bandaged his wounds, carried him to safety, and ensured he was cared for. That was a burden. It was real. It was powerful. It required action.

But the Samaritan did not move into the inn and turn roadside rescue into his lifelong assignment.

A calling is different. A calling shapes your life. That distinction is crucial in church planting because church planting is not sustained by enthusiasm alone. It is sustained by conviction.

Church planting may look exciting from a distance, but anyone who has done it knows that it includes long nights, emotional strain, financial uncertainty, and difficult seasons when progress seems painfully slow.[2]

Enthusiasm cannot carry you through those moments. Calling can.

When God Will Not Let You Go

Moses teaches us this clearly. He spent forty years in Midian before the burning bush. When God called him, Moses did not immediately embrace the assignment. He resisted. He questioned. He argued. He even tried to redirect God toward someone else. "Who am I, that I should go unto Pharaoh?" (Exodus 3:11).

Moses was not eager. He was reluctant. But when God calls, He knows how to get a person's attention.

My spiritual father, Bob McCool Sr., experienced something similar. Early in his ministry, he started a church in Johnson City, Tennessee, in the beautiful Appalachian region near the Smoky Mountains. It was a wonderful place to live. The scenery was breathtaking. The streams were clear. It was the kind of place many people would gladly choose to stay forever.

But God began dealing with him about going to West Memphis, Arkansas. West Memphis was not Johnson City. It did not offer mountain streams and cool breezes. It offered humidity, heat, and the muddy Mississippi. Naturally, he resisted.

Then something unusual happened. He became seriously ill and was hospitalized. The doctor told him he would receive medicine and should soon improve, but somehow the medicine never came. Day after day passed, and still no medicine arrived. Finally, lying in that hospital bed, he understood that God was dealing with him.

In that quiet room, he surrendered. "Okay, God. I will go." And as the story has been told for years, the healing he needed came at that moment. He got dressed, checked out of the hospital, and prepared to obey God.

That story reminds me of something we all eventually learn: God knows how to deal with our resistance. He knows how to bring us to the place where surrender becomes the only path to peace.

Confirmation, Submission, and Response

Samuel's story adds another important layer. In 1 Samuel 3, the voice of the Lord was rare in those days. Yet God called a boy. Samuel did not recognize the voice at first. He thought Eli was calling him. Three times he ran to Eli, saying, "Here am I; for thou calledst me" (1

Samuel 3:5). Finally, Eli perceived what was happening and instructed Samuel to respond, "Speak, Lord; for thy servant heareth" (1 Samuel 3:9).

Samuel had the call, but he needed guidance to recognize it.

Calling often requires mentorship. Not everything spiritual is immediately obvious. Not every impression is instantly clear. God often uses spiritual authority and wise counsel to help confirm what He is saying.[3]

That is why I strongly believe that if you are married, your spouse must be involved in discerning God's call. If your spouse does not share peace about what you believe God is saying, the answer is not to bulldoze ahead. It may be that your timing is off. It may be that more prayer is needed. In the same way, your pastor must be involved. Spiritual authority is not a hindrance to calling. It is often one of the ways God confirms it.

Calling and Submission Work Together

I once heard about a gifted minister who had served faithfully as his pastor's right-hand man for years. He began feeling called to plant a church in a nearby city. He approached his pastor, but the pastor did not initially feel peace about it. The minister did not become resentful. He did not pull away. He kept serving. Faithfully.

As time passed, the pastor began to sense that the call really was from God. Eventually, he approached the minister and said he believed God was indeed calling him and his wife to plant that church. The minister smiled and said, "Pastor, I never could get away from planting that church. But I told God that if I was supposed to go, He would speak to you, and you would come to me."

That is how things should be done. Calling and submission are not enemies. They are partners.

There are, in my view, three dimensions to every church-planting call. First, there is the mission. Jesus came "to seek and to save that which was lost" (Luke 19:10). That mission belongs to every believer. Second, there is the commission, the specific place, people, or field God assigns to you. Third, there is submission, because mission and commission become dangerous when disconnected from authority, accountability, and spiritual covering.[4]

The centurion in Matthew 8 understood this. He told Jesus, "I am a man under authority" (Matthew 8:9). That statement caught Jesus' attention. He marveled at it. Why? Because the centurion understood that authority only works when it is connected to submission. Church planters must understand that same principle.

Spiritual authority flows through spiritual alignment.

Ordinary People, Extraordinary Calling

Throughout all of this, one truth keeps surfacing: God still calls ordinary people to extraordinary assignments. Jesus did not build His movement by choosing the religious elite. He called fishermen. He called tax collectors. He called common men. And He simply said, "Follow me, and I will make you fishers of men" (Matthew 4:19).[5]

He did not tell them to make themselves into something. He told them to follow Him. And He promised He would do the forming.

You may feel unqualified. You may feel intimidated by the city, the culture, or the scale of the need. But if you follow Him, He will make you into what the assignment requires.

When Obedience Rearranges a Life

My bishop, D. D. Davis, embodied this kind of obedience. He had planted a thriving church in Texas. Life was going well. The church was growing. He had built a new home. They had horses. By every outward measure, life was strong and blessed. Then God called him to Long Island, New York.

That was not a minor adjustment. That was a radical call. To leave Texas for Long Island meant leaving the familiar for the unfamiliar, the comfortable for the challenging, the known for the unknown. It meant trading predictability for uncertainty.

And he obeyed.

Because he obeyed, a gospel witness was planted in one of the world's most significant regions. That is how church planting works. God calls. Someone obeys. A church is born. It sounds simple. But anyone who has walked that path knows it is anything but easy.

The Call That Changes Everything

Looking back on our own journey, I can say with confidence that calling changes everything. It changes how you see cities. It changes how you define success. It changes what you are willing to sacrifice. Once God places a city in your spirit, you do not look at maps the same way. You do not hear population statistics the same way.

Once God places a city in your spirit, you start seeing souls where others see skylines. You start sensing responsibility where others feel only sympathy.

That is what happened to me on that plane over New York. A city got into my spirit. And once that happened, everything afterward became part of answering one question: Was I willing to say yes?

That is the real question behind every church-planting call. Not, "Do I fully understand it?" Not, "Can I guarantee success?" Not, "Will it be easy?" But simply: Will I obey?

Because every pioneer eventually reaches a point where no further information is needed. What is required is not more clarity. It is more surrender.

Scripture shows us this pattern again and again. Abraham had to go. Moses had to answer. Samuel had to listen. Isaiah had to respond, "Here am I; send me" (Isaiah 6:8). The disciples had to leave their nets. Every time God extended His kingdom, someone had to step into the unknown.

That has not changed. God calls. People respond. The Kingdom advances.

Perhaps that is where you are as you read this chapter. Maybe you have felt something stirring that you cannot explain. Maybe a city keeps coming to your mind. Maybe a county, a neighborhood, or a community keeps resurfacing in your spirit. Maybe it is not random. Maybe it is not emotional. Maybe it is not temporary.

Maybe God is doing more than stirring your heart. Maybe He is calling you.

If that is true, then you are standing in a sacred tension. Calling creates a question, and that question demands a response. You can acknowledge it and move forward. Or you can ignore it and hope it fades. But calling rarely fades. It waits. It lingers. It returns in quiet moments. It surfaces in prayer. It stays with you because it is not just an idea.

It is an invitation.

Talk to your spouse. Pray together. Seek peace, not pressure. Talk to your pastor. Invite counsel, not just confirmation. Submit your spirit. Let God confirm what He is saying. But do not dismiss what He is doing either.

Because when God calls, He does not merely offer an interesting option. He extends an invitation that can redefine an entire life. And eventually, every church planter must answer that call, not with words, but with action.

The Response That Defines You

Sometimes the moment that changes everything does not appear life-changing. It does not happen in a crowded sanctuary. It does not come with applause or a spotlight. Sometimes it happens quietly, in a conversation, in a prayer, in a decision no one else sees.

For me, it started in a darkened airplane, looking out a window, while God let a city get in my spirit. But that moment was not the end. It was the beginning. Because hearing the call is not the same as answering it. A burden may stir the heart. But a response still has to be made.

And that is where the journey truly begins.

The call of God always leads to a crossroads. If God is still calling people to reach cities, neighborhoods, and communities, then the question becomes unavoidable: Who will go? Once God places a city in your spirit, the issue is no longer about discernment.

The issue becomes response.

Discussion & Application

Use these questions for personal reflection or group discussion.

1. The author describes a moment on an airplane when a city "got in his spirit." Have you ever experienced a moment where God placed a specific place or people on your heart in a way you could not shake? How did you respond, and what did you learn about yourself in that process?

2. The chapter distinguishes between a burden and a calling; one is seasonal, the other enduring. How can a leader practically discern which one they are experiencing? What guardrails would you put in place before acting on what feels like a calling?

3. The story of the minister who told God, "If I'm supposed to go, You'll speak to my pastor, and he'll come to me," illustrates the relationship between calling and submission. In what ways does your current ministry culture encourage or hinder that kind of trust in spiritual authority?

4. The chapter presents three dimensions of a church-planting call: mission, commission, and submission. Which of these three is most overlooked or undervalued in your ministry context? What would it look like to strengthen it?

5. D. D. Davis left a thriving church in Texas because God called him to Long Island. What is the most difficult thing God could ask you to leave behind in order to obey a church-planting call? What would it take for you to say yes?

Chapter Three

Someone Has to Respond

In the early morning hours of March 13, 1964, a young woman named Kitty Genovese was returning home to her apartment in Queens, New York. It had been an ordinary evening. The city had settled into the quiet rhythm that only appears after midnight. Streetlights reflected off parked cars. Apartment windows glowed faintly as people slept inside.

Then the silence was shattered.

Kitty was attacked and killed just outside her apartment building. She cried out for help in the darkness. The story that followed would become one of the most discussed events in modern social psychology. Early reports claimed that dozens of people heard her cries but failed to intervene. Later investigations showed the situation was more complex than headlines first suggested. Some neighbors did attempt to help. Others were unsure what they were hearing amid the early-morning confusion.

Yet the story revealed something deeply troubling about human behavior. Psychologists studying the incident eventually gave a name to the phenomenon they believed had occurred.[1]

They called it the bystander effect.

The bystander effect describes what happens when many people witness a crisis but assume someone else will respond. Instead of one person stepping forward immediately, responsibility becomes diffused among the crowd. Someone else will call the police. Someone else will intervene. Someone else will handle the situation.

And when everyone assumes someone else will act, sometimes no one does.

The larger the crowd, the easier it becomes to stand still. Researchers have studied the bystander effect in countless settings since that night in Queens. They discovered something fascinating: the presence of more witnesses often reduces the likelihood that any one person will take action. If many people see the problem, surely someone else will solve it. If others are present, surely someone more qualified will step forward.

At first glance, that tragedy may seem like a distant event from another era. But the deeper lesson reaches far beyond a single street in New York. It reveals something about human nature. When responsibility is shared by many people, it often becomes owned by no one. Everyone assumes someone else will respond. And while the crowd hesitates, the moment for action quietly slips away.

The Church and the Bystander Effect

That same dynamic can quietly appear in the mission of the church. Entire communities can remain without a gospel witness, not because the church does not care, but because everyone assumes someone else will go.

Across America and around the world, there are communities filled with people who have never encountered an Apostolic church. Entire counties exist where the message of Acts 2:38 is rarely heard. Apartment complexes house thousands who have never had a Bible study in their living room. College campuses overflow with students searching for truth but never encountering a Spirit-filled witness.

The need is enormous.

When everyone assumes someone else will go, sometimes no one does. And the city waits.

Yet it is surprisingly easy, even for sincere believers, to assume someone else will respond. Someone else will plant the church. Someone else will move to that city. Someone else will start the Bible study. Someone else will reach that neighborhood. Someone else will answer the call.

When D. D. Davis heard the story of Kitty Genovese, it deeply affected him. The idea that so many people could witness a crisis and yet fail to respond troubled him, not only as a commentary on society, but as a mirror for the church.

As he reflected on the story, a phrase began to form in his heart. Somebody has to help. Somebody has to respond. Someone has to care. Those words were not merely commentary on a tragic event. They became a spiritual conviction. Entire cities could remain spiritually underserved simply because everyone assumed someone else would go.

But what if no one did?

The bystander effect does not only occur on city streets. It can quietly creep into the mission of the church. And when it does, cities that desperately need the gospel simply continue waiting, not because no one cares, but because no one accepts the responsibility as their own.

When the Burden Becomes Personal

Church planting rarely begins with a strategic planning meeting. Most of the time, it begins quietly. A city begins appearing repeatedly in prayer. A region starts weighing heavily on the heart. A community that once felt distant suddenly feels personal.

At first, the feeling may seem like compassion. But over time, the burden deepens. The thought begins to form: maybe this is more than concern. Maybe this is responsibility. That realization can be unsettling. Surely someone else could do this better. Surely someone more experienced should go. Surely someone else will respond.

But movements of God rarely begin with people who feel fully qualified. They begin with people who simply choose to obey.

Before there was a nation called Israel, there was a man named Abraham who left everything familiar because God called him to go (Genesis 12:1). Before Israel was delivered from bondage, a shepherd named Moses stood before a burning bush (Exodus 3:2–10). Before there was a prophetic voice calling Israel back to righteousness, a boy named Samuel learned to hear the voice of God in the night (1 Samuel 3:10). Before the gospel spread across the Roman world, fishermen left their nets when Jesus said two words: "Follow Me" (Matthew 4:19).

Crowds rarely start movements. Individuals do.

One of the most important leadership principles for church planters is this: Kingdom movements begin when responsibility becomes personal. As long as the need belongs to someone else, nothing changes. When the need becomes personal, obedience begins.[2]

Nehemiah rebuilt the walls of Jerusalem because the burden became personal (Nehemiah 2:17–18). Paul planted churches across the Roman world because the mission became personal (Acts 13:2–3). Every revival movement in history began when someone decided the responsibility belonged to them.

The Harvest Was Never the Problem

When Jesus looked at the crowds that followed Him, He saw something many around Him did not. Others saw inconvenience. Others saw interruption. Others saw problems.

Jesus saw harvest.

Matthew records that Jesus looked at the multitudes and was moved with compassion because they were weary and scattered like sheep without a shepherd. Then He made a statement that still defines the mission of the church: "The harvest truly is plenteous, but the labourers are few" (Matthew 9:37).

Those words deserve careful attention. Notice what Jesus did not say. He did not say the harvest was small. He did not say people were uninterested. He did not say revival was impossible. He said the laborers were few.

The harvest has never been the problem. The shortage has always been responders.

For church planters, this is a liberating realization. Many leaders worry that the culture has become too resistant to the gospel. They assume people are uninterested or spiritually closed. But Jesus saw the situation differently. The fields are ready.[3]

The question has never been whether people are hungry for truth. The question is whether someone will go into the field and gather the harvest.

Compassion Must Lead to Action

Compassion is a powerful emotion. It is what moves us when we see suffering, injustice, or spiritual darkness. But compassion alone is not enough to change a city.

Compassion must eventually lead to action.

Jesus did not merely feel compassion for the crowds. He preached to them, healed them, taught them, and ultimately commissioned His disciples to reach them. Nehemiah did not merely weep over the broken walls of Jerusalem. He traveled there and rebuilt them himself (Nehemiah 1:3–4). Paul did not merely feel compassion for the lost cities of the Roman world. He traveled thousands of miles planting churches and preaching the gospel (Acts 16:9–10).

Compassion that does not lead to action fades into sentiment. Compassion that leads to obedience changes history.

This is one of the most important leadership lessons a church planter can learn. Feeling the burden is only the beginning. At some point, the burden must translate into movement. Prayer must turn into preparation. Concern must turn into commitment. Vision must turn into action.[4]

God Works Through Availability

At some point, every believer must answer a simple but life-defining question. Will I remain a spectator? Or will I respond? Because somewhere today, there is a city waiting for a church. Somewhere there is a neighborhood waiting for someone to knock on the door with a Bible study chart. Somewhere there is a campus filled with students searching for truth. And somewhere there is a church planter wrestling with the same question that echoed through Isaiah's temple: "Whom shall I send, and who will go for Us?" (Isaiah 6:8).

The future of a city may depend on the answer.

Why Many People Hesitate

For most church planters, there is a moment when the burden stops being theoretical and becomes personal. Sometimes that moment happens during prayer. A particular city keeps coming to mind and refuses to go away. Sometimes it happens during a conversation with a pastor or mentor who sees something in a leader that they may not yet see in themselves.

At that moment, the church planter realizes something profound. The responsibility might actually belong to them. That realization is both inspiring and intimidating. It means the call of God is no longer something to admire from a distance. It is something to obey.

One of the most common reactions to that realization is hesitation. Church planting feels enormous. It involves relocating families, starting ministries from scratch, raising financial support, and building relationships in unfamiliar communities. For many leaders, the assignment feels larger than their experience.

The internal dialogue begins quickly. I am not ready. I do not have the resources. Someone else could do this better. Surely there are more qualified people. These thoughts are not new. They appear repeatedly throughout Scripture.

When God called Moses to lead Israel out of Egypt, Moses immediately offered reasons he was the wrong person (Exodus 4:10–13). When God called Jeremiah, Jeremiah protested that he was too young (Jeremiah 1:6). When God called Gideon, Gideon insisted he came from the weakest family in the weakest tribe (Judges 6:15).

Yet in every one of those stories, God did not deny the leader's limitations. He simply promised His presence. The success of the mission would not depend on their ability. It would depend on their obedience.

God rarely chooses people based on their credentials. He chooses people based on their availability.

The world evaluates leaders by résumé. God evaluates leaders by willingness. Throughout Scripture, the pattern is consistent. God chooses ordinary people who are willing to obey and then accomplishes extraordinary things through them.[5]

Fishermen became apostles (Matthew 4:18–20). A shepherd boy became a king (1 Samuel 16:11–13). A tax collector became an evangelist (Luke 5:27–28). A persecutor of the church became the apostle Paul (Acts 9:3–6).

The kingdom of God advances when ordinary people make themselves available to an extraordinary God.

The Courage to Begin Small

One reality every church planter must embrace is that great churches rarely begin in impressive settings. Most church plants begin in living rooms, storefronts, rented school auditoriums, or borrowed facilities. The early days can feel fragile. Attendance may fluctuate. Resources may feel limited. Progress sometimes appears slow.

But small beginnings should not discourage us. They should remind us how the kingdom of God works.

Jesus compared the kingdom to a mustard seed, small, almost insignificant, but over time it grows into something that influences an entire environment (Matthew 13:31–32). Church planting follows that same pattern. Faithfulness in the early days builds the foundation for what comes later. The church planter's responsibility is not to guarantee rapid growth. It is to remain faithful to the calling.

The Generational Impact of One Church

The impact of a single church often extends far beyond what anyone initially imagines. When a church is planted in a community, it begins influencing not only the people who attend immediately but also the generations that follow. Children grow up hearing the Word of God. Families find restoration. Young people discover purpose and calling.[6]

Those young people grow into adults who shape the future of their communities. A church that begins with ten people in a living room can eventually influence thousands of lives across decades. When you plant a church, you are not simply starting a congregation.

You are planting a spiritual legacy.

That reality changes how we view the sacrifices involved in church planting. The long hours, the financial uncertainty, and the emotional challenges become investments in something that will outlive us. Church planting is not merely about the present. It is about the future. Cities grow. Communities expand. Populations shift. New generations rise. Without new churches being planted, the gospel's presence in those communities can slowly fade.

Church planting keeps the light shining in new places.

Every church that exists today began with someone who was willing to take a step of faith. Every congregation began as a church plant. Every revival story started with a beginning that probably felt small and uncertain at the time. Church planting is not simply a denominational strategy. It is a kingdom necessity.

The City That Is Still Waiting

Every generation inherits a moment of responsibility. For some believers, that moment comes quietly during prayer. For others, the moment arrives during a missions service or a leadership gathering where the needs of a particular region become impossible to ignore.

However it arrives, the moment always carries the same realization: the responsibility might belong to me. The city is no longer an abstract dot on a map. It suddenly has faces. Families. Children growing up without ever hearing the gospel clearly explained. Neighborhoods where brokenness has become normal, and hope feels distant.

At that moment, the question that once sounded theoretical becomes deeply personal. Who will go?

The Power of One Response

The tragedy that unfolded in Queens in 1964 forced an uncomfortable conversation about human behavior. Psychologists explained it through the bystander effect. Responsibility becomes diluted when shared by many people. Everyone assumes someone else will act.

But the deeper lesson from that night is this: a crisis only continues until someone finally decides to step forward. The moment one person calls for help, the moment one person intervenes, the moment one person accepts responsibility, everything begins to change. That principle applies directly to the mission of the church.

Across our world, there are cities waiting for someone to respond. Neighborhoods where the gospel is rarely heard. Communities where brokenness has become normal, and hope feels distant. And sometimes the danger is not opposition. The danger is assumption. Someone else will plant the church. Someone else will move to that city.

But when everyone assumes someone else will go, the city continues waiting. Until one person finally says yes.

History is filled with moments when one person's response changed everything. Abraham responded when God said go (Genesis 12:1). Moses responded when God called from the burning bush (Exodus 3:10). Samuel responded when he heard the voice of God in the night (1 Samuel 3:10). Isaiah responded, "Here am I; send me" (Isaiah 6:8). The disciples left their nets. Before there was a thriving church in Antioch, someone had to preach the gospel there first (Acts 11:20–21). Before there were believers meeting in Philippi, someone had to cross the sea (Acts 16:9–10).

Crowds rarely start movements. Responders do.

Every revival movement in history began when someone decided the responsibility belonged to them. Every church that exists today began with someone who heard the call and said yes. Church planting has never been about perfect circumstances. It has always been about obedient people.

"I Started with a Calling"

Years ago, a small congregation gathered in a rented space to begin what would eventually become a thriving church. At the beginning, there were only a handful of people. The pastor preached to a room that felt far too empty. Some weeks, the offering barely covered expenses. Discouragement threatened to overwhelm the vision.

But the pastor kept preaching. The small group kept praying. Bible studies continued. Slowly, lives began to change. One family was restored. Then another. Young people began discovering their calling. Children who grew up in that church eventually became pastors, missionaries, and church planters themselves.

Years later, someone asked the pastor if he had ever imagined the influence that church would eventually have. He smiled and said something simple: "I didn't start with a crowd. I started with a calling."

And that is how every church begins. Not with certainty. But with obedience.

The Question That Still Echoes

The harvest fields of our world are enormous. Jesus looked at the crowds and said, "The harvest truly is plenteous, but the labourers are few" (Matthew 9:37). The harvest has never been the problem. The shortage has always been responders.

And so the question that echoed through Isaiah's temple continues to echo today: "Whom shall I send? And who will go for Us?" (Isaiah 6:8). Somewhere today, a city is waiting for someone to answer that question. Perhaps the burden you feel is not accidental. Perhaps the reason that city keeps appearing in your prayers is that God placed it there.

Movements of God rarely begin with crowds. They begin when someone responds.

Responding to the call of God is a powerful moment, but it is only the beginning of the journey. Calling ignites the vision. Preparation sustains the mission. Before a church planter launches a new congregation, God often spends years shaping the leader's spiritual life, character, relationships, and practical wisdom.

Hearing God's voice may happen in a moment. Preparing for the assignment takes a lifetime.

Discussion & Application

Use these questions for personal reflection or group discussion.

1. The bystander effect describes how responsibility becomes diluted when shared by many people. In what specific ways have you seen this dynamic play out in the church's approach to unreached communities? What would it look like to disrupt that pattern in your context?

2. The chapter argues that compassion without action fades into sentiment. Think about a burden God has placed on your heart in the past. Did it lead to concrete action, or did it gradually fade? What made the difference?

3. Moses, Jeremiah, and Gideon all hesitated when God called them, yet God did not deny their limitations; He simply promised His presence. What limitations or inadequacies do you most often use to justify delay? How does God's promise of presence challenge that reasoning?

4. The pastor in the closing story said, "I didn't start with a crowd. I started with a calling." What is the difference between launching from certainty and launching from calling? How does that distinction change the way you evaluate readiness for church planting?

5. If your leadership team conducted an honest assessment of the unreached communities within driving distance of your church, what would you find? What would it take for your church to move from awareness of the need to ownership of the responsibility?

Part 2: The Preparation

*"**F**or we are his workmanship, created in Christ Jesus unto good works, which God hath before ordained that we should walk in them" (Ephesians 2:10).*

"The deeper God wants to use you, the longer He tends to prepare you." - Rick Warren

Chapter Four

Preparing the Church Planter

On December 17, 1903, two bicycle mechanics from Dayton, Ohio, changed the course of human history. Wilbur and Orville Wright launched a fragile wooden aircraft into the cold winds above the sand dunes of Kitty Hawk, North Carolina. The flight lasted just twelve seconds. The plane traveled only 120 feet. Yet those twelve seconds forever altered the trajectory of human transportation.

What most people never consider is that the Wright brothers did not stumble into success overnight. That first flight was the visible result of years of hidden preparation. They studied bird flight patterns and built wind tunnels. They conducted hundreds of glider experiments. They failed repeatedly and crashed more than once. They adjusted designs, recalculated angles, and refined their understanding of lift, thrust, and balance.[1] For years, it looked like nothing was happening. But something was happening. Those brothers were preparing.

Long before the airplane left the ground, the groundwork for flight had already been laid.

The same principle applies to church planting. Most people celebrate the visible moments of ministry. The launch service. The first revival. The first baptisms. The first building purchased. But long before any of those moments appear, preparation must take place. Church planting rarely begins with a public service. It usually begins in quiet seasons where God shapes the future planter long before the work becomes visible.

Preparation is the runway that allows ministry to take flight. Without it, the plane never leaves the ground.

Preparation Before Commission

Scripture repeatedly shows us that God prepares His servants long before He releases them into their assignments. This is not an accident. It is a divine pattern. God does not rush the development of the people He intends to use. He shapes them in secret. He refines them in obscurity. And He often does His deepest work in seasons when no one else is watching.

Moses spent forty years in the wilderness tending sheep before he ever confronted Pharaoh (Exodus 3:1). Not forty days. Forty years. Those years were not wasted. God was shaping his character, cultivating patience, and deepening his dependence. Every sunburn and sleepless night in that desert was preparation for the palace. The shepherd's staff had to come before the miracle rod.

David experienced a similar process. Long before he wore the crown of Israel, he spent years tending sheep in the lonely fields of Bethlehem (1 Samuel 16:11). Those fields became the training ground where David learned to trust God and developed the courage to confront Goliath. The lion and the bear came before the giant. The field came before the throne.

Even the apostle Paul experienced a season of preparation. After his conversion on the Damascus Road, he did not immediately assume global leadership. He spent significant time in relative obscurity before beginning his missionary ministry (Galatians 1:17–18).[2] God was not wasting Paul's time. He was forging Paul's theology, deepening his dependence, and preparing him for the rigors of Apostolic ministry.

God often prepares leaders in hidden places before He positions them in visible ones.

Church planters must understand this rhythm. Calling may come suddenly, but preparation usually takes time. And the depth of the preparation often determines the durability of the ministry. A church planter who launches too quickly without adequate preparation may possess passion, but passion alone cannot sustain a church plant for the long haul. God often spends years preparing a leader for a work that may begin with a single service.

Do not despise the hidden season. Do not rush through the preparation. What God is building in you during that season is the very thing that will hold you together when the pressures of ministry come. And they will come.

The Five Areas of Preparation

When God calls someone to plant a church, the call itself is only the beginning of the journey. A church planter must be prepared across multiple dimensions of life before launching a new congregation. Over years of observing successful church planters, I have noticed that preparation typically occurs in five critical areas: spiritual, relational, emotional, ministerial, and financial.

Each of these areas contributes to the long-term health of the church planter and the church they will eventually lead. Neglect one, and the work can suffer. Develop them well, and the foundation becomes strong enough to sustain the pressures of ministry. Let me walk through each one, because understanding these areas could mean the difference between a ministry that endures and one that burns out before it ever reaches its potential.

Spiritual Preparation

Spiritual preparation is the most important dimension of all. Church planting is not simply an organizational project. It is a spiritual mission. The church belongs to God. Jesus said, "I will build my church; and the gates of hell shall not prevail against it" (Matthew 16:18). Notice the emphasis carefully. Jesus did not say, "You will build the church." He said, "I will build my church." Church planters are not architects. They are participants in a work that God Himself is building.

Because of that reality, spiritual formation must come before strategic planning. Future church planters must cultivate a life of prayer. They must develop a deep relationship with Scripture. They must learn to recognize the voice of God.[3] The spiritual depth required to lead a church cannot be manufactured overnight. It grows gradually through consistent, unhurried time in the presence of God. You cannot shortcut the process. You cannot microwave what God intends to slow-cook.

Church planters must learn to pray bold prayers long before they stand behind a pulpit. Prayer births vision. Prayer sustains endurance. Prayer protects humility. Without deep spiritual preparation, ministry eventually becomes mechanical. But when spiritual preparation runs deep, ministry flows from an authentic, living relationship with the God who called you.

You cannot give away what you do not possess.

Relational Preparation

Church planting also requires relational preparation. Ministry does not happen in isolation. Church planters must learn how to build healthy relationships with people. They must develop trust with mentors, pastors, and spiritual leaders who provide guidance and accountability.[4] No one plants a church alone. And no one should try.

The New Testament repeatedly emphasizes the importance of spiritual relationships. Paul mentored Timothy. Barnabas encouraged younger leaders. The early church functioned as a community rather than a collection of isolated individuals. Healthy relationships provide wisdom during difficult seasons, encouragement when ministry becomes discouraging, and accountability when decisions grow complex.

Church planters who ignore relational preparation often struggle unnecessarily. Those who cultivate strong relationships find themselves supported by a network of wisdom and encouragement that carries them through the hardest days. The ones who thrive are the ones who invest in relationships long before the pressures of ministry demand them.

Emotional Preparation

Church planting demands emotional resilience. Starting a church can be exhilarating, but it can also be emotionally draining in ways you never anticipated. There will be moments of celebration and moments of deep disappointment. Attendance fluctuates. Finances diminish. People sometimes leave without warning. Criticism surfaces when you least expect it. Emotionally healthy leaders are better equipped to navigate these realities without becoming discouraged or defensive.

The apostle Paul understood this balance well. He wrote, "I know both how to be abased, and I know how to abound: every where and in all things I am instructed both to be full and to be hungry, both to abound and to suffer need. I can do all things through Christ which strengtheneth me" (Philippians 4:12–13). Paul's strength did not come from favorable circumstances. His strength came from deep, daily dependence on Christ.

Leadership is not sustained by adrenaline. It is sustained by stability.

Leadership carries emotional weight that is hard to describe until you carry it yourself. When someone in the congregation is hurting, the pastor feels that burden. When finances are limited, the pastor carries that concern. When conflict arises, the pastor must navigate the tension with grace and wisdom. No church planter should attempt to carry these demands alone. Healthy friendships, trusted mentors, and supportive family members provide stability during the hardest seasons.

Emotional health is not weakness. It is wisdom.

Ministerial Preparation

Church planters must also develop ministerial competence. Ministry involves more than preaching sermons. It requires shepherding people, organizing teams, solving problems, and guiding a congregation through complex decisions. Future church planters benefit greatly from serving in existing churches before launching their own works. Serving as youth pastors, assistant pastors, evangelists, or ministry leaders provides invaluable experience in pastoral care, leadership development, and church administration.

Kenneth Carpenter once summarized ministry with a simple but powerful statement: "Ministry is doing anything that it takes to make the local church successful." Jesus modeled this pattern with His disciples. Before sending them into the world, He spent years allowing them to observe His ministry firsthand. They watched Him teach crowds, heal the sick, respond to critics, and care for individuals.

Leadership is often caught rather than taught. Church planters must learn to serve before they lead.

Those hidden seasons of service provide the practical experience that sustains a church plant for the long term. The future pastor who has cleaned bathrooms, set up chairs, taught Bible studies, and served wherever needed develops a deep appreciation for the work of ministry. Those experiences build the kind of humility that sustains long-term leadership. Preparation may feel slow, but it is never wasted. The runway must be long enough before the plane can take off.

Financial Preparation

One area of preparation that is frequently overlooked is financial stewardship. Church planting requires faith, but faith does not eliminate the need for wisdom. Responsible financial preparation removes obstacles that might otherwise hinder the mission. And a powerful example of this principle is the story of Donny and Ashley Willis.

While he was a student at Texas Bible College, God gave him a vivid dream. In the dream, he saw a massive steel globe, the Unisphere, standing outside the USTA Billie Jean King National Tennis Center in Queens, New York. At the time, he had never even heard of the Unisphere. Yet the image burned into his spirit. That dream became the beginning of their call to the New York City metro area.

At first, the Willises believed they would plant a church in College Point, New York, near LaGuardia Airport and Citi Field. The burden for New York settled deeply into their hearts. Then God began moving pieces that only He could arrange. When the Lord called my family and me to return to Memphis to pastor Faith Apostolic Church, it became clear that the Willises were God's choice to lead the church we had started in Westchester County, New York.

Years earlier, Carlton Coon had introduced me to Donny Willis at General Conference when he was still a Bible college student. None of us realized at the time that the young man standing there would eventually become my successor in Westchester. Today, that church continues to flourish under his leadership. But the most important part of their story is not simply that they were called. It is how they prepared for the call.

After graduating from Bible college, the Willises served faithfully as student pastors in two churches in Louisiana. They poured themselves into ministry, gaining valuable pastoral experience. At the same time, they made a deliberate financial decision that many young ministers overlook. They chose discipline over debt. They lived carefully. They avoided unnecessary financial obligations. They saved aggressively. Little by little, month by month, they built a financial foundation that would eventually make their move possible.

By the time the door opened to relocate to New York, they had positioned themselves to step into their calling with stability rather than desperation. Their financial stewardship allowed them to purchase a home in one of the most expensive regions in the United States and begin ministry without crushing financial pressure. That kind of preparation is not accidental. It is intentional.[5]

Donny and Ashley Willis understood something every church planter must learn. Calling and stewardship must walk together. Faith does not eliminate wisdom. Trust in God does not replace preparation. Their story is a model for every aspiring church planter. It proves that financial preparation and spiritual obedience are not enemies. They are partners. The Willises did not wait for perfect conditions. They created conditions that allowed them to obey when the moment arrived.

Sometimes the greatest act of faith is managing your finances well enough that when God says go, you are actually able to go.

Removing Obstacles to Obedience

Financial preparation is not about becoming wealthy before obeying God. It is about removing obstacles to obedience. Church planters who prepare financially are not less spiritual. They are more responsible. Responsible stewardship protects the mission. It allows leaders to make decisions based on calling rather than financial desperation.

Financial preparation means knowing your numbers. It means reducing unnecessary debt and creating a realistic family budget. It means having honest conversations with your spouse about the financial realities of church planting. It means preparing for seasons when the church may not yet fully support the pastor. Most importantly, it means recognizing that financial stewardship is part of spiritual maturity.

Jesus spoke frequently about money because financial decisions often reveal the condition of the heart. Church planters who handle finances wisely create stability not only for themselves but also for the families they lead and the congregations they will eventually serve. When the moment arrives to step into the calling, the prepared church planter is ready to move.

The Character That Sustains the Calling

Talent may attract attention. Charisma may inspire crowds. Vision may ignite momentum. But character sustains the work.

The apostle Paul instructed Timothy with these words: "Take heed unto thyself, and unto the doctrine; continue in them: for in doing this thou shalt both save thyself, and them that hear thee" (1 Timothy 4:16). Notice the order carefully. Paul first told Timothy to pay attention to himself. Before doctrine. Before preaching. Before ministry activity. Character comes first.

Church planters must guard their integrity with everything they have. Their personal life, family relationships, and spiritual disciplines form the unseen structure that holds the ministry together. When character weakens, the structure begins to crack. When character remains strong, the ministry stands firm. People follow leaders who demonstrate emotional consistency and spiritual maturity.[6]

Talent opens doors but character determines how long you stay in the room.

The goal of church planting is not simply to launch a church. The goal is to build something that continues to impact lives long after the planter's initial excitement fades. Paul described the Christian life as a race: "I have fought a good fight, I have finished my course, I have kept the faith" (2 Timothy 4:7). Ministry is not a sprint. It is a marathon.

The emotional, spiritual, and relational preparation that happens before launching a church often determines whether a leader can sustain the work for decades. History is filled with stories of leaders who started strong but did not finish well. Church planters must adopt the mindset that finishing matters more than starting. Every church planter eventually encounters moments when the mission feels impossibly difficult.

Paul encouraged weary believers with these words: "And let us not be weary in well doing: for in due season we shall reap, if we faint not" (Galatians 6:9). That verse contains a promise. Harvest follows perseverance. But perseverance requires preparation. God rarely asks leaders to be extraordinary. He asks them to be faithful.

From Preparation to Connection

When the Wright brothers launched their airplane at Kitty Hawk, the moment lasted only seconds. But that flight represented years of preparation. The same principle holds true for church planting. A church launch may take place in a single service, but the strength of that church often depends on years of faithful preparation in the life of the planter.

Spiritual preparation deepens the leader's relationship with God. Relational preparation builds supportive connections. Emotional preparation strengthens resilience. Ministerial preparation develops practical skills. Financial preparation removes obstacles to obedience. Together, these five areas create a foundation strong enough to sustain the mission.

But preparation alone is not enough. Eventually, every church planter discovers a deeper truth. The mission cannot be sustained through preparation alone. It must be sustained through connection. Connection with God. Connection with the source of spiritual life. The church is not ultimately built by strategy. It is sustained by the Spirit of God and established through the Word of God.

The church is God's idea. He is both the originator and the sustainer. God will not conceive something in the Spirit and then expect us to bring it to life through human strength alone. What God births in the Spirit must be sustained by the Spirit. That truth changes everything.

It reminds us that preparation may position us, but connection sustains us. Preparation may open doors, but connection keeps them open. Preparation may start the work, but only a living connection with God can sustain it.

That reality leads us to the next critical principle: church planters must learn to remain deeply connected to the source of spiritual power.[7] That connection is not optional. It is the lifeline of the mission. Without it, ministry becomes mechanical. With it, ministry becomes supernatural. It flows from prayer. It flows from intimacy with God. It flows from a heart that stays tender before the Lord, even when the work gets hard.

If that relationship is not healthy and growing, all the church-planting techniques in the world will never produce a lasting work. Over the next four chapters, we will explore the power of our relationship with God and how it shapes our faith, expands our vision, develops our character, and fuels our expectation for what He can do through us. As the health of the church planter goes, so goes the church.

Church planting is more than setting up and tearing down equipment. It is more than launch teams, systems, and strategy. The true life of a church plant flows from the spiritual health of the planter.

Before God builds something through you, He will build something in you.

Discussion & Application

Use these questions for personal reflection or group discussion.

1. The chapter identifies five areas of preparation: spiritual, relational, emotional, ministerial, and financial. Which of these five do you believe is most often neglected by aspiring church planters in your context? What are the practical consequences of that neglect, and how have you seen it play out in real ministry situations?

2. Donny and Ashley Willis chose discipline over debt for years before relocating to New York. What specific financial decisions would you need to make today to position yourself for obedience when God opens a door? What obstacles currently stand in the way, and what is your plan to address them?

3. Paul told Timothy to take heed to himself before taking heed to doctrine (1 Timothy 4:16). Why is that order significant for church planters? In what ways can the pressure to perform in ministry cause leaders to neglect their own spiritual and emotional health? How do you guard against that tendency in your own life?

4. The chapter argues that "leadership is often caught rather than taught." What practical steps can an aspiring church planter take to maximize the learning available in their current ministry role, even if they are not yet in a senior leadership position? What lessons have you personally learned by serving before leading?

5. The closing section warns that church planters fail not from lack of strategy but from loss of connection with God. What practices or rhythms would you build into your weekly life to protect that connection during the demanding early years of a church plant? How would you hold yourself accountable to maintaining them when the pressures of ministry intensify?

Chapter Five

Staying Connected to the Source

I glanced down at my phone and noticed the dreaded red battery icon. It had been a long day. Calls. Messages. Emails. Navigation. Somewhere along the way, I had forgotten the most important part of keeping the phone functioning.

Charging it.

The phone itself was still impressive. The screen worked. The apps were still installed. The hardware was intact. But none of that mattered once the battery drained. Without power, the phone became little more than a sleek paperweight. It still looked functional. But it was not.

That small moment illustrates a truth every church planter must learn early in ministry: function requires connection to a source. A phone disconnected from power eventually dies. A branch disconnected from the tree eventually withers. A hand severed from the body cannot survive.

And a minister disconnected from God will eventually lose spiritual power.

Church planting places enormous demands on a leader. Vision must be cast. People must be discipled. Sermons must be prepared. Facilities must be secured. Outreach must be organized. Problems must be solved. All of these responsibilities are real. But none of them matter if the church planter loses connection to the source of spiritual life.

Two Biblical Pictures of Connection

Scripture illustrates the importance of connection through powerful imagery. In John 15, Jesus describes the relationship between Himself and His followers using the picture of a vine and its branches. "I am the vine, ye are the branches: He that abideth in me, and I in him, the same bringeth forth much fruit: for without me ye can do nothing" (John 15:5). The branch does not produce fruit on its own. It receives life from the vine. Everything the branch needs flows through that connection.

Apart from Him we can do nothing. Not less. Nothing.

Another powerful picture appears in 1 Corinthians 12, where Paul describes the church as a human body. Hands, feet, eyes, and ears all function differently, yet they remain connected to the same body. If one part becomes disconnected, it cannot survive on its own. A severed hand cannot perform the tasks it once accomplished. Connection is not optional. It is essential for life.

These images reveal something crucial for church planters. Ministry is not sustained by talent. It is sustained by connection. The church is God's idea, not ours. He conceived it, He sustains it, and He empowers it.[1]

God will never conceive something in the Spirit and allow us to accomplish it through the flesh.

If the Spirit birthed it, the Spirit must sustain it. That truth alone can save a church planter from a thousand foolish burdens. You are not trying to prop up a human invention. You are partnering with a divine work. Church planters must work hard, plan wisely, and lead faithfully. But none of those things can replace abiding in Christ.

Contact Is Not Connection

During my years serving as a youth pastor in West Memphis, Arkansas, I was once asked to move a trailer using the church van. I carefully backed the van toward the trailer hitch and believed I had connected everything properly. At least, I thought I had.

As I drove through a neighborhood a few minutes later, I glanced in the mirror and experienced a moment of absolute horror. The trailer was traveling beside the van at roughly the same speed.

The van had made contact with the trailer. But it had never actually connected.

Thankfully, no one was hurt, and no property was damaged. But the lesson stuck with me. The same principle applies spiritually. Many people have moments of contact with God. They attend a powerful service. They feel moved during worship. They experience a moment of conviction during preaching. Those encounters matter. But encounters are not the same as connection.

An encounter with God can create a memory. A connection with God creates transformation.

That distinction is especially important in church planting because ministry can create the illusion of connection. Leaders can spend so much time around spiritual things that they begin assuming proximity equals intimacy. They preach sermons, lead services, attend meetings, and pray publicly. Yet it is entirely possible to be surrounded by ministry and still be drifting from God.[2]

Some leaders are near the trailer. They have even bumped into it. But they have never truly locked in.

Jesus used a very specific word in John 15 to describe the relationship He desires. He said, "Abide in me, and I in you. As the branch cannot bear fruit of itself, except it abide in the vine; no more can ye, except ye abide in me" (John 15:4). The word abide means to remain, to dwell, to continue in an ongoing relationship. Jesus was not describing a momentary experience. He was describing a lifestyle.

Church planters who attempt to lead without abiding eventually discover that their spiritual reserves run dry. Vision alone cannot sustain ministry. Charisma cannot sustain ministry. Strategy cannot sustain ministry. Only connection to God can sustain ministry over the long haul.

The church planter who abides in Christ draws strength from a place deeper than emotion. They are not merely surviving on yesterday's sermon, last month's conference, or a memorable altar service from years ago. They are living in present-tense dependence upon God. They are learning to let the life of Christ flow into their thinking, priorities, speech, and leadership.

Abiding is more than a devotional concept. It is a ministry necessity.

This truth becomes even more important in the cultural moment we are living in today. Paul warned Timothy about the spiritual climate of the last days: "This know also, that in the last days perilous times shall come" (2 Timothy 3:1). Leadership in ministry has never been simple. But in an age of constant information, social media pressure, and cultural hostility toward biblical conviction, the demands placed on church leaders continue to intensify.

The solution is not simply working harder. It is staying connected deeper.

The Engine of Prayer

If connection to God is the lifeline of ministry, then prayer is the primary way to maintain that connection. Many leaders think of prayer as preparation for ministry. They pray before preaching. They pray before meetings. They pray before making important decisions.

Prayer is not merely preparation for the battle. Prayer is the battle.

The real spiritual work of ministry often happens long before a sermon is preached or a Bible study is taught. It happens in quiet places where leaders seek God and intercede for the people they are trying to reach. Church planters who understand this principle approach prayer differently. They see it as the spiritual engine that powers everything else.

When prayer weakens, ministry weakens. When prayer strengthens, ministry strengthens.

"Old Camel Knees"

One of the most powerful biblical voices on prayer came from James the Just, the brother of Jesus and a leader in the early church in Jerusalem. Early Christian historians tell us that James spent so much time in prayer that his knees developed thick calluses from kneeling. Believers gave him a strange but memorable nickname.

They called him "Old Camel Knees."

When he wrote about prayer in his epistle, people listened carefully. "The effectual fervent prayer of a righteous man availeth much" (James 5:16). James was not describing polite religious language spoken during church services. He was describing persistent, heartfelt intercession that reaches heaven and changes outcomes on earth.

James strengthens his point by pointing to Elijah. "Elias was a man subject to like passions as we are, and he prayed earnestly that it might not rain: and it rained not on the earth by the space of three years and six months. And he prayed again, and the heaven gave rain, and the earth brought forth her fruit" (James 5:17–18). Elijah experienced fear, exhaustion, and discouragement. Yet through prayer, he saw extraordinary answers from God.

Prayer connected human weakness with divine power. That same connection is available today.

Church planters often look at the cities they are called to reach and feel overwhelmed. The needs are great. The spiritual resistance is real. The obstacles can appear enormous. But prayer introduces a new factor into the equation. When leaders pray, heaven moves. Prayer does not remove every obstacle overnight. But it invites the power of God into situations where human ability is insufficient.

"Give Me Scotland"

History provides powerful examples of leaders who understood the power of prayer. The Scottish reformer John Knox lived during a time of political chaos and spiritual corruption. Yet he believed God could transform the nation. His prayer became legendary: "Give me Scotland, or I die."[3]

This was not the arrogant demand of a proud man. It was the desperate cry of someone whose heart burned for the salvation of his people. Knox prayed with such intensity that even the queen took notice. Mary, Queen of Scots, reportedly said she feared the prayers of John Knox more than all the assembled armies of Europe.[4]

A queen feared a praying preacher more than military power. Because spiritual authority flows from connection with God.

The Hidden Intercessor

Another remarkable example appears in the ministry of Charles Finney. Finney's preaching sparked revivals across large regions of the United States. Entire communities experienced astounding moral transformation. Bars closed. Crime dropped. Churches filled.

But behind the scenes, another man played a crucial role. His name was Daniel Nash. Nash devoted himself to intercessory prayer. When Finney scheduled a revival meeting, Nash would travel there weeks in advance. He would rent a small room and spend days praying for the city. Witnesses reported hearing him groan and weep in prayer as he asked God to pour out the Spirit on the community.

When Nash sensed a release in his spirit, he would send word to Finney that the town was ready. Finney would arrive, begin preaching, and revival would erupt. When Daniel Nash died, Finney soon stopped traveling as an evangelist. He believed something essential had been lost.

The engine of prayer had been removed. History remembers the preacher. But heaven also remembers the intercessor.

The Chair

Prayer does not always begin with dramatic revival stories. Sometimes it begins with something very simple. A chair.

A businessman once told his pastor he did not have time to pray. The pastor responded gently that people usually find time for what matters most. The comment lingered. Soon, the man began waking earlier each morning. He would carry his coffee and Bible to a chair in his home and spend time reading Scripture and talking with God. He began referring to that place simply as "the chair."

Over time, his thinking changed. His priorities changed. Eventually, he told his pastor that, with his approval, he would like to retire from his business and help support a new church plant in another state. When the pastor asked where these ideas were coming from, the man smiled and said, "The chair."

Starting his day in the chair revolutionized everything. His life. His work. His ministry. His family. His marriage.

Prayer changes people before it changes circumstances.

Church planters who develop daily places of prayer, whether a chair, a desk, a study, or a quiet room, create sacred spaces where God shapes their hearts and guides their decisions. Prayer anchors the church planter's connection with God. But prayer alone does not sustain that connection. The Word of God also plays a crucial role. Prayer allows us to speak to God. Scripture allows God to speak to us.

The Word, the Fast, and the Flow of Life

Prayer keeps the church planter connected to God through conversation. Scripture keeps the church planter connected through truth. A church planter who neglects Scripture eventually discovers that the pressures of ministry begin to shape their thinking instead of the voice of God.

The Bible does far more than provide sermon material. It forms the inner life of the leader. The psalmist wrote, "Thy word have I hid in mine heart, that I might not sin against thee" (Psalm 119:11). The Word of God protects the life of the believer. It guards the mind. It steadies the heart. It anchors conviction when cultural pressure intensifies.

Church planters operate in environments where spiritual resistance is real. Cities are filled with competing ideas, moral confusion, and spiritual darkness. Without a deep foundation in Scripture, leaders can gradually absorb the assumptions of the culture around them. But when the Word lives in the leader's heart, it becomes a stabilizing force. It becomes the compass.

What You Are Made of Matters

On April 15, 1912, the RMS Titanic struck an iceberg in the North Atlantic and sank, taking more than 1,500 lives. In 1991, researchers recovered a piece of the hull and examined the metal scientifically. What they discovered surprised many experts. The steel was extremely brittle. When the ship struck the iceberg, the metal did not bend inward. It fractured. Like broken china.[5]

The real issue was not simply the collision. The real issue was what the ship was made of.

The same principle applies spiritually. The pressures of ministry eventually reveal what a leader is made of. Criticism will come. Discouragement will come. Unexpected challenges will arise. When those moments arrive, the leader's inner life becomes critical. If the Word of God has been deeply embedded in the heart, the leader bends without breaking.

Jesus demonstrated Scripture's power during His temptation in the wilderness. Three times the enemy presented a temptation. Three times Jesus answered with the same phrase: "It is written" (Matthew 4:4, 7, 10). The Word of God became the weapon that defeated the enemy's attack. Church planters will face spiritual opposition. When that resistance appears, the Word of God becomes one of the most powerful defenses available.

The Power of Fasting

If prayer connects the leader to God and Scripture strengthens the mind, fasting intensifies spiritual authority. Throughout Scripture, fasting appears repeatedly during moments when God's people faced serious spiritual resistance. Jesus assumed His followers would fast. "Moreover when ye fast, be not, as the hypocrites, of a sad countenance" (Matthew 6:16). He did not say if. He said when.

Fasting humbles the body and sharpens spiritual sensitivity. It reminds the leader that true strength comes from dependence upon God, not physical resources. A fellow church planter once told me something I have never forgotten: "If you want to break something in the spirit in your city, go on a three-day fast. If you want to break something in the spirit in your nation, go on a seven-day fast. If you want to break something in the spirit in the world, go on a twenty-one-day fast."

At first, that statement sounded dramatic. But experience has confirmed the principle. Fasting weakens the influence of the flesh and strengthens spiritual authority. It positions the leader to hear God more clearly and confront spiritual resistance more effectively. Many church planters have discovered that seasons of fasting often precede major spiritual breakthroughs in their cities.

Fasting also creates a holy desperation that reshapes the leader's dependence on God. When the body feels weak, the spirit becomes alert. When physical appetite is set aside, spiritual hunger intensifies. The leader who fasts regularly develops a sensitivity to the Spirit that cannot be achieved through study or strategy alone.

When the Springs Dry Up

In the early 1800s, a family traveling along an old stagecoach road stopped for the night because their baby had fallen ill. While resting in nearby woods, they discovered several natural springs. They bathed the child in the cool water, and by the next morning, the child had recovered. Stories about the springs began to spread.

Travelers came to "take the waters." A grand hotel was built. Music played in ballrooms. High society gathered for rest and healing. The area became known as Raleigh Springs, a community that still exists today in Memphis, Tennessee.

But something changed. The underground water table dropped. The springs dried up.

When the water disappeared, the crowds stopped coming. The grand hotel remained for a while, but without the springs, the attraction vanished. Eventually, the property declined, and the buildings burned. The name remained. But the springs were gone.

The tragedy of Raleigh Springs was not sudden. No one noticed the day the water level began to drop. The decline was gradual. Quiet. Invisible at first. By the time the absence became obvious, the damage had already been done. The same quiet decline threatens every ministry that stops drawing from the source.

Church history contains many similar stories. Churches that once experienced vibrant spiritual life sometimes slowly lose their connection to the source. Programs may remain. Buildings may remain. Traditions may remain. But the springs dry up. And when the springs dry up, the ministry loses its life.

Church planters must guard against that possibility from the very beginning.

Returning to John 15, branches receive three things from the vine: provision, purpose, and production. Provision means the life of the branch flows from the vine. Purpose means the branch exists to produce fruit. Production means the branch actually bears that fruit over time. If the branch becomes disconnected, all three disappear.

Disconnection leads to decline. Connection leads to fruit.

The only way a church planter can remain effective from the launch of a church until the return of Christ is by staying connected to the source. Prayer. Scripture. Fasting. These disciplines keep the springs flowing. They sustain the leader's life and the church's health.

Without them, ministry becomes exhausting. With them, ministry becomes fruitful.

Church planting begins with a calling, but it is maintained by connection. And the church planter who stays connected to the source will discover something remarkable over time. The same power that birthed the church will preserve the church.

Every church planter eventually discovers that staying connected to God shapes more than personal spirituality. It also shapes the way we think. The mind becomes one of the most important battlegrounds in ministry. Thoughts influence attitudes. Attitudes influence actions. Actions influence outcomes.

If church planters are going to lead healthy churches, they must learn to win the battle that takes place between their ears.

Discussion & Application

Use these questions for personal reflection or group discussion.

1. The chapter distinguishes between "contact" and "connection" with God. In what ways can the busyness of ministry create the illusion of spiritual connection while the leader is actually drifting? What warning signs would you look for in your own life?

2. The story of Daniel Nash reveals that the power behind Finney's revivals was sustained intercession. Who is praying behind the scenes for your church plant or ministry? What would it look like to intentionally build a prayer team that functions as the spiritual engine of your work?

3. The Titanic illustration argues that what you are made of determines whether you break under pressure. What specific spiritual disciplines are you building into your inner life right now that will support you when criticism, discouragement, or unexpected challenges arrive?

4. The chapter presents prayer, Scripture, and fasting as three lifelines of spiritual connection. Which of these three is strongest in your current practice, and which is weakest? What is one concrete step you could take this week to strengthen the weakest area?

5. The Raleigh Springs story warns that the name and the structures of a church can remain long after the spiritual life has dried up. How can a church planter build accountability structures that will honestly signal when the "springs" of their ministry are beginning to fade?

Chapter Six

Choose Life

I f you have ever read *The Lord of the Rings*, you know that J. R. R. Tolkien did far more than tell a story. He built a world. He imagined rivers and mountains, kingdoms and histories, languages and alliances. He gave us the warmth of the Shire, the beauty of Rivendell, the menace of Mordor, and the courage of men standing at Helm's Deep. Middle-earth feels real because Tolkien saw it before he wrote it.[1]

The world existed in his mind before it ever existed on paper.

That is true of every meaningful creation. It exists in the mind before it exists in reality. Now raise that truth to its highest level. Tolkien created a fictional world through imagination and language. God created the actual world through His mind and His mouth. Genesis does not begin with God gathering raw materials or consulting outside experts. It begins with God. "In the beginning God created the heaven and the earth" (Genesis 1:1).

Then, in the midst of darkness and disorder, "And God said, Let there be light: and there was light" (Genesis 1:3). Hebrews 11:3 adds, "Through faith we understand that the worlds were framed by the word of God, so that things which are seen were not made of things which do appear."

Creation began in the mind of God and came forth through the mouth of God.

That principle matters deeply for the church planter. Before a church takes shape in a city, it begins taking shape in the inner life of its leader. Before there is a congregation, there is a way of thinking. Before there is a culture in the church, there is a culture in the mind. Before people hear the leader's voice in the pulpit, they will eventually feel the world that leader has been building in their thoughts.

In many ways, a church planter is always building two worlds at once: the inner world no one sees and the congregational world everyone will eventually feel.

That is why Deuteronomy 30 is such an important text for leaders. Moses stood before Israel and said, "See, I have set before thee this day life and good, and death and evil" (Deuteronomy 30:15). Then he pressed the point further: "I have set before you life and death, blessing and cursing: therefore choose life" (Deuteronomy 30:19). The passage is about covenant obedience, but it also reveals a broader spiritual principle. Life rarely drifts accidentally in the right direction. It is chosen. It is shaped by what we love, what we obey, what we hold onto, and what we continually rehearse.

Every church planter must learn that their future congregation will be deeply affected by two things that help determine their destiny: their mind and their mouth.

Renewing the Mind: The Neglected Discipline

One of the great neglected disciplines in the modern church is biblical meditation. Part of the reason is that the culture has borrowed the word and filled it with meanings foreign to Scripture. Because false religions and secular self-help movements have popularized their own forms of meditation, some Christians have backed away from the biblical practice altogether. But abandoning a biblical discipline because the world has distorted it is never wisdom. It is surrender.

Biblical meditation is not emptying your mind. It is filling your mind with the right thing. It is not detaching from reality. It is anchoring yourself in reality as God defines it. It is not retreating into self. It is turning toward the Word of God until your mind begins to think God's thoughts after Him.

That is why Joshua 1:8 says, "This book of the law shall not depart out of thy mouth; but thou shalt meditate therein day and night." Notice the connection between mind and mouth. The Word remains in your mouth because it has first been planted in your mind. The Hebrew idea behind meditation includes pondering, muttering, rehearsing, and speaking quietly to oneself.[2]

Biblical meditation is not passive. It is active. It is the deliberate practice of turning truth over in your mind until it begins shaping how you think, feel, and live.

The psalmist understood this well. "O how love I thy law! it is my meditation all the day" (Psalm 119:97). Paul gives Timothy the same instruction: "Meditate upon these things; give thyself wholly to them; that thy profiting may appear to all" (1 Timothy 4:15). In Philippians 4:8, Paul tells believers to think on whatever is true, honest, just, pure, lovely, and of good report. That is not random advice for positive thinking. It is discipleship for the mind.

Church planters need that discipleship desperately.

Because if you do not choose what fills your mind, your city, your critics, your fears, and your cultural moment will choose for you. A church planter who constantly feeds on anxiety will begin leading anxiously. A church planter who constantly rehearses offense will begin leading offensively. A church planter who constantly dwells on scarcity will eventually speak as though scarcity is lord.

But a church planter who learns to meditate on the Word of God will begin thinking differently. And different thinking will eventually shape different leading. Romans 12:2 says, "And be not conformed to this world: but be ye transformed by the renewing of your mind." Transformation begins in the invisible world before it shows up in the visible world. Long before the church planter changes a congregation, the Spirit of God must change the way the church planter thinks.

You cannot consistently lead people beyond the world you live in mentally.

If your mind is full of defeat, your church will feel it. If your mind is full of fear, your team will sense it. If your mind is renewed by truth, strengthened by Scripture, and shaped by faith, your people will feel that too. That does not mean the church planter becomes unrealistic. It means they become governed by a higher reality. They are not ignoring facts. They are refusing to let facts have the final word.

They are learning to interpret the visible through the lens of the invisible. They are learning to say, "This city may be hard, but God is faithful. This season may be uncertain, but the Word of God is sure. We may be small, but the kingdom of God has always loved mustard seeds." That kind of thinking does not happen by accident. It is cultivated. It is rehearsed. It is chosen.

And that is exactly why Moses said, "Choose life." Before life becomes visible in the congregation, it must be chosen in the leader's inner world. Church planting is not merely a matter of location, strategy, and opportunity. It is also a matter of imagination sanctified by Scripture. The church planter must learn to think in agreement with God before they can speak in agreement with God.

Because eventually, what fills the mind will flow through the mouth. And when it does, it will begin shaping the world around them.

The Atmosphere Your Mouth Creates

If the mind is the architect of the church planter's inner world, the mouth is the builder that sets that world into motion. That is not dramatic language. It is biblical language. Proverbs 18:21 says, "Death and life are in the power of the tongue." That is not merely poetic flourish. It is spiritual reality.

That is especially important for a church planter, because a new congregation is fragile in the early days. People are still learning how to think about the mission, how to interpret setbacks, and how to see their place in the story God is writing. In that formative season, the planter's words carry unusual weight. Their speech helps create the emotional and spiritual atmosphere of the church.

In many ways, the church planter's mouth becomes a thermostat. It helps set the temperature in the room.

If their speech is filled with anxiety, fear begins spreading through the congregation. If their speech is cynical, suspicion begins settling in the culture. If their speech is harsh, people begin guarding themselves instead of opening their hearts. But if their speech is marked by faith, grace, truth, and hope, those qualities begin to shape the church as well.

James understood the disproportionate power of the tongue. He wrote, "Even so the tongue is a little member, and boasteth great things. Behold, how great a matter a little fire kindleth!" (James 3:5). He then says, "And the tongue is a fire, a world of iniquity" (James 3:6). Something very small can set something very large ablaze.

A spark can burn a forest. A rudder can steer a ship. A tongue can shape a church.

We are not God. We do not create universes by speaking. But we are made in His image, and because of that, our words carry delegated influence. We do not speak with divine sovereignty, but we do speak with real consequence. Our words help shape relationships, expectations, direction, and culture. They reveal what fills the heart, and they reinforce what a people begin to believe.

Jesus made that point clearly in Luke 6:45: "Out of the abundance of the heart the mouth speaketh." The mouth is diagnostic. It tells on the heart. If a church planter's speech is constantly filled with negativity, sarcasm, or complaint, that is not merely a communication problem. It is a heart problem surfacing through speech. If their words consistently carry life, peace, courage, and grace, that too reveals something about the interior world from which they are living.

Spiritual growth is not merely about saying nicer things. It is about becoming the kind of person whose heart has been shaped by God.

The Nails and the Fence

There is an old story about a boy who struggled with anger. His father told him to hammer a nail into a fence every time he said something hurtful. At first, the nails went in quickly. Over time, as the boy learned to control his speech, the number decreased. Then the father told him to remove one nail for every kind word he spoke. Eventually, the nails were gone. But the father took him back to the fence and said, "The nails are gone, but the holes remain."

Some words leave holes. Church planters must never forget that.

In the formative season of a church, one bitter comment from the leader can damage morale. One dismissive remark can diminish a volunteer. One pattern of venting can create a culture of complaint. One sarcastic tone can train a church to become critical instead of compassionate. But the reverse is also gloriously true.

Words can heal.

Proverbs 12:18 says, "There is that speaketh like the piercings of a sword: but the tongue of the wise is health." Proverbs 16:24 adds, "Pleasant words are as an honeycomb, sweet to the soul, and health to the bones." Ephesians 4:29 tells believers, "Let no corrupt communication proceed out of your mouth, but that which is good to the use of edifying, that it may minister grace unto the hearers."

A church planter's words should become beams, not wrecking balls.

Paul does not merely say, "Avoid bad language." He says speak what is necessary for edification. Let your words build. Let them strengthen. Let them impart grace. A math teacher once asked her students to write down the nicest thing they could think of about each classmate. She compiled the comments and gave each student a page of affirming words. Years later, one of those students was killed in Vietnam. At his funeral, the teacher learned he had carried that folded page in his wallet. Other former students revealed they had kept their pages in drawers, diaries, and wedding albums.

The words had outlived the classroom. That teacher had given them something to carry.

Church planters should speak that way. Their words should become something people can carry into Monday, into trouble, into temptation, into grief, and into growth.

The Word in Your Heart and the Sword in Your Hand

By now, we have seen two foundational truths. First, the mind shapes the inner world of the leader. What fills the mind eventually shapes the direction of ministry. Second, the mouth releases influence into the environment. What the leader repeatedly speaks begins forming the culture of the church. But there is a third dimension that connects the mind and the mouth together: the Word of God.

Without the Word, the mind drifts. Without the Word, speech becomes opinion instead of authority. Without the Word, the leader's inner world slowly begins to conform to the culture around them rather than to the kingdom within them. This is why Scripture repeatedly returns to the central role of God's Word in the believer's life.

When believers meditate on Scripture, they are not merely memorizing information. They are internalizing truth until it begins shaping the imagination, the emotions, the decisions, and ultimately the language of their lives. Transformation begins with renewed thinking. And renewed thinking eventually produces renewed speaking.

That is why the Word of God becomes the foundation of spiritual warfare as well as spiritual growth.

The Sword of the Spirit

Paul describes the believer's spiritual armor in Ephesians 6. Most of the pieces he lists are defensive: the helmet of salvation, the breastplate of righteousness, the shield of faith, the shoes of the gospel. But one piece of equipment is offensive. One weapon allows the believer not merely to endure the enemy's attacks but to confront them.

Paul writes, "And take the helmet of salvation, and the sword of the Spirit, which is the word of God" (Ephesians 6:17). The Greek word translated sword is *machaira*, a short, razor-sharp weapon designed for close combat. Unlike the large ceremonial swords used in parades, the *machaira* was practical and deadly. It was designed to strike quickly and precisely at close range.[3]

But Paul adds another important detail. The word he uses for "word" in this verse is not *logos*, the general term for the written Word of God. Instead, he uses *rhēma*, which refers to a specific word quickened by the Spirit for a particular moment.

A *rhēma* word almost always emerges from the reservoir of *logos* already stored in the believer's heart.

The sword of the Spirit does not appear magically out of thin air. It comes from a life immersed in Scripture. It comes from meditation. It comes from storing the Word of God in the mind until the Holy Spirit can draw from that reservoir in the moment it is needed.

The Two-Mouthed Sword

This explains why the Word of God is sometimes described as a two-edged sword. Hebrews 4:12 says, "For the word of God is quick, and powerful, and sharper than any twoedged sword." The phrase translated "two-edged" comes from the Greek word *distomos*, which literally means two-mouthed.[4]

One edge of the sword comes from the mouth of God. The second edge comes when that Word comes out of the mouth of the believer. When God first spoke His Word, it carried divine authority. But when that same Word is believed, internalized, and spoken by a believer, it becomes a two-mouthed sword. The same truth that came from heaven now echoes through the voice of a disciple.

That is why Jesus defeated temptation in the wilderness not by arguing with the devil but by quoting Scripture. Three times, He answered the adversary with the same phrase: "It is written" (Matthew 4:4, 7, 10). The Word in His mouth became a weapon in His hand.

Church planters must learn the same discipline. Ministry inevitably involves seasons of spiritual pressure. Discouragement whispers that the work is pointless. Fear suggests that the city is too hard. Comparison insists that other ministries are succeeding faster. Accusation whispers that you are not qualified, not capable, not ready.

In those moments, the mind must be anchored in truth, and the mouth must respond with truth.

When a leader says, "God is faithful," they are not reciting a slogan. They are wielding a weapon. When they declare, "The gates of hell shall not prevail against it" (Matthew 16:18), they are not quoting poetry. They are reinforcing reality. When they proclaim, "For all the promises of God in him are yea, and in him Amen" (2 Corinthians 1:20), they are reminding themselves and their people that God's purposes do not depend on favorable circumstances.

Words of faith become weapons against lies.

From Discipline to Dependence

Over time, a church planter who meditates on Scripture begins speaking Scripture naturally. Their prayers become saturated with the language of the Bible. Their preaching becomes rooted in the promises of God. Their private conversations begin reflecting the tone of heaven instead of the tone of the culture. And when that happens, the atmosphere of the church begins changing. Faith grows. Hope spreads. People begin believing that God can actually do what He has promised.

In many ways, that is how movements begin. A leader spends enough time with God that their thinking changes. Their speech begins reflecting that transformation. And slowly, the people around them begin adopting the same perspective. One story captures this beautifully. When Walt Disney World opened in 1971, Walt Disney had been dead for five years. His brother Roy oversaw the project's completion. During the dedication, someone reportedly said, "It's a shame Walt isn't here to see this." Roy replied, "He did see it. That's why it's here."[5]

Disney World existed in Walt's imagination long before it existed in Florida. Vision always begins internally.

Church planting works the same way. Before a thriving congregation appears in a city, a leader must see something others cannot yet see. Before people gather in the room, someone must believe that they will gather. Before revival comes, someone must begin praying and speaking as though revival is possible. That is why the disciplines of thinking and speaking in alignment with God's Word matter so much. They shape the unseen world where vision is born.

Every day, the church planter faces the same decision Moses placed before Israel: "I have set before you life and death, blessing and cursing: therefore choose life" (Deuteronomy 30:19). Choose life in what you think. Choose life in what you speak. Choose life in what you rehearse when no one else is listening. Over time, those choices create an atmosphere where faith grows stronger than fear, and hope speaks louder than doubt.

When a leader begins shaping that kind of atmosphere, a church can begin growing in ways that strategies alone could never produce. Before a church is built in a city, it is built in the inner life of the church planter. The mind must be renewed. The mouth must be governed. The Word must be internalized and spoken. Because long before a leader stands before people, they have already been shaping the world those people will step into.

The Edge of Ability

But there is a tension every church planter eventually feels. You can think right. You can speak right. You can fill your heart with the Word of God. And still come face-to-face with something you cannot produce. You cannot make revival happen. You cannot force hunger in people. You cannot guarantee growth, response, or fruit.

At some point, every church planter reaches the edge of their own ability and realizes that disciplined thinking and careful speech, while essential, are not enough.

They prepare the ground. They do not send the rain. This is where faith enters the story. What the mind believes and what the mouth speaks must ultimately be anchored in something greater than personal discipline. They must be anchored in confidence in God. The renewed mind helps you see rightly. The guarded mouth helps you speak rightly. But faith is what enables you to move forward when nothing visible confirms what you believe.

Faith is what allows a church planter to stand in an empty room and still see it filled. Faith is what keeps them preaching when the response is small. Faith is what sustains them when results are slow and resistance is strong. In many ways, this chapter has been about alignment, bringing the inner life into agreement with God.

Because at the end of the day, church planting is not maintained by mindset alone. It is preserved by faith.

Discussion & Application

Use these questions for personal reflection or group discussion.

1. The chapter argues that a church planter is always building two worlds, an inner world and a congregational world. What specific practices are you using right now to build a healthy inner world, and where do you see the greatest vulnerability in your thought life as a leader?

2. Moses told Israel to "choose life." In what practical ways can a church planter choose life through the discipline of biblical meditation, especially when circumstances are producing fear, discouragement, or comparison?

3. The chapter describes the leader's mouth as a thermostat that sets the temperature of the church. Think about the last month of your leadership. What temperature has your speech been creating in the people around you, and what would need to change?

4. Paul distinguishes between *logos* (the written Word) and *rhēma* (a quickened word for a specific moment). How have you experienced the Holy Spirit bringing a specific Scripture to your mind during a moment of spiritual pressure, and how did it affect the outcome?

5. The chapter ends by acknowledging that disciplined thinking and careful speech still cannot produce revival. How does a church planter balance the responsibility to renew the mind and govern the mouth with the reality that only God can send the rain?

Chapter Seven

Bless Me Indeed

I n 1904, a young Welsh coal miner felt a weight that refused to lift. His name was Evan Roberts. He was twenty-six years old. He had no platform, no denominational backing, and no reputation as a preacher. He had coal dust under his fingernails and a burden in his spirit. For thirteen years, he had prayed for revival in Wales. Most of those prayers were whispered in mine shafts and bedrooms. No one applauded them. No one recorded them. Heaven was the only audience.

Then, in the autumn of that year, Roberts prayed a dangerous prayer. It was not polished. It was not strategic. It was four words long. "Bend me, O Lord." That was it. He did not ask for a pulpit. He did not ask for a crowd. He asked to be bent until every stubborn part of him surrendered. He prayed it again and again. Something broke. Something opened. And heaven came down on a nation.

Within months of that prayer, more than one hundred thousand people became Christians across Wales. Taverns emptied. Crime dropped so sharply that judges arrived at court with no cases to try. Coal miners who had cursed the mules underground began teaching the animals new commands because the old ones had been profane. Entire communities were transformed. Not by a polished leader. Not by a gifted orator. By a yielded life that dared to pray a different kind of prayer.

History remembers movements. Heaven remembers the man or woman who dared to ask.[1]

Every church planter eventually faces the same crossroads Roberts faced. Will you pray safe prayers that protect your comfort? Or will you pray bold prayers that enlarge your capacity?

The future of your ministry will not be determined by your vision alone. It will be determined by the size of the prayers you are willing to pray.

The Gap Every Planter Lives In

Every church planter carries a quiet tension. On one hand, there is vision. You see a thriving church where there is currently nothing. You imagine lives changed and families restored. You see a baptistry stirred with new birth. You hear worship filling a room that does not yet exist.

On the other hand, there is reality. You cannot manufacture revival. You cannot force hunger into hearts. You cannot guarantee every outreach will bear fruit. You cannot control God's timing or a city's openness. Sooner or later, you stand in the gap between what you see in your spirit and what you see with your eyes.

Sometimes that moment hits in an empty sanctuary. Sometimes it hits over financial numbers that do not add up. Sometimes it hits late at night, when the adrenaline has worn off, and the weight settles in. And a question arises. Can God really do something significant here, through me?

That is not a small question. It is the question. Most planters do not struggle with whether God can do great things in general. They believe that. They preach that. The deeper struggle is personal. Can God do it in this city, with these people, through my leadership, within my limits? That is where faith stops being theology and becomes survival.

Every church begins the same way. Not with a building. Not with a crowd. Not even with a launch team. It begins with something invisible. A burden. A stirring. A word from God. Scripture says, "Through faith we understand that the worlds were framed by the word of God, so that things which are seen were not made of things which do appear" (Hebrews 11:3).

Light existed in the heart of God before it existed in the universe. Order existed in His mind before it appeared in creation. That same pattern still holds. Before a church exists in a city, it exists in the heart of God. Before it gathers in a building, it exists in the spirit of a leader who heard Him speak. Church planting is not starting something new. It is partnering with something God already envisioned.

Faith That Sees Before It Sees

Hebrews gives us one of the clearest definitions of faith in all of Scripture. "Now faith is the substance of things hoped for, the evidence of things not seen" (Hebrews 11:1). Faith gives substance to what does not yet exist. Faith treats future promises as present realities. Faith lets a planter preach to people not yet in the room, pray for disciples not yet baptized, and prepare for growth not yet arrived.

You begin setting chairs before they are needed. You train leaders before you have a crowd. You build systems before there is pressure. Because faith sees it before it sees it. If you only respond to what you currently see, your ministry will always lag behind what God wants to do. But if you respond to what He has spoken, you position yourself ahead of what is coming.

Noah built an ark when there was no rain (Hebrews 11:7). Abraham left home without knowing where he was going (Hebrews 11:8). Moses chose suffering with God's people over comfort in Egypt (Hebrews 11:25). None of them had visible proof when they started. They had a word. And that was enough. Hudson Taylor, the pioneer missionary to China, captured this conviction when he said, "There are three stages to every great work of God: impossible, difficult, done."[2]

Church planting lives in that same tension. You are building something that, for a long season, only you and God can see. And that is enough.

The Real Battle Is Confidence

If there is one thing the enemy targets in a church planter, it is not personality. It is not gifting. It is confidence. Hebrews warns, "Cast not away therefore your confidence, which hath great recompence of reward" (Hebrews 10:35). Why would Scripture warn us not to throw away confidence? Because pressure makes you want to.

Slow growth makes you question. Financial strain makes you hesitate. Opposition makes you reconsider. Fatigue makes you wonder if you heard God correctly. Confidence is not loud. It is not arrogance. It is not self-promotion. Confidence is a quiet conviction that says, God spoke, and I still believe Him.

The enemy rarely convinces a planter to quit outright. He simply convinces them to settle. To lower expectations. To shrink vision. To stop asking boldly. But Hebrews follows that warning with a promise. "For ye have need of patience, that, after ye have done the will of God, ye might receive the promise" (Hebrews 10:36). There is always a gap between obedience and fulfillment. Faith lives in that gap.

John Maxwell once said, "Everything rises and falls on leadership."[3] But before leadership rises publicly, confidence must rise privately. If you lose confidence in what God said, you will eventually settle for what you can manage.

Hebrews 11 reads like a hall of faith, but it is not a list of flawless people. Noah struggled. Abraham lied out of fear. Jacob manipulated his way through life before God changed him. These were not perfect people. They were persistent people. They stayed. They endured. They kept believing. God is not looking for perfection. He is looking for faithfulness. Faithfulness over time creates fruit.

When Faith Must Become Prayer

At some point, every planter must move from believing God can do it to asking God to do it. Faith that never turns into prayer eventually becomes frustration. Because you will see what should be happening, but you will not experience the power to bring it to pass. Prayer is where faith finds its voice. It is where vision stops being internal and becomes relational.

Right in the middle of a long genealogy, where most readers would normally skim, God pauses the record to highlight one man and one prayer. It is almost as if heaven leans in and says, Do not miss this. "And Jabez was more honourable than his brethren: and his mother called his name Jabez, saying, Because I bare him with sorrow" (1 Chronicles 4:9). Before we ever hear what he prayed, we learn who he was. He was honorable. Not famous. Not powerful. Not influential yet. But he had weight. Substance. Character.

The Life That Should Have Stayed Small

In 1820, in a small New York community, a baby girl was born into circumstances that seemed to promise a limited life. Within weeks, a medical mistake took her sight. Within months, death took her father. Her name was Frances Jane Crosby, later known as Fanny Crosby. If you had looked at her early life, you would not have predicted global influence.

You would have seen restriction, dependency, and loss.

Yet something happened. She refused to let her condition become her conclusion. Over time, she began to write. Not a few songs. Thousands. Conservative estimates place her output above eight thousand hymns. "Blessed Assurance." "Pass Me Not, O Gentle Savior." "Rescue the Perishing." She never saw the congregations singing her songs. She never saw sunlight filtering through stained glass as believers lifted their voices.[4]

And yet, from a life that seemed painfully restricted, God brought astonishing enlargement. Her words crossed oceans. Her hymns filled sanctuaries. Her influence outlived her lifetime. What others called a closed life, God turned into an open field. When asked if she regretted her blindness, she replied that if she could be granted one wish, it would be to remain blind. Her reason? "When I get to heaven, the first face that shall ever gladden my sight will be that of my Saviour."

Your beginning may explain you, but it does not have to define you.

Some lives begin under the sign of pain. Jabez knew that. Fanny Crosby knew that. And if we are honest, many planters know that as well. Not every planter begins with ideal conditions. Some are still fighting names the past tried to give them. Not enough. Too inexperienced. Too late. Too small. But Jabez reminds us of something powerful. Your beginning does not determine your destiny.

Jabez refused to let his past become the boundary of his future. Planters must do the same.

He Called on God

The turning point in the text comes in one phrase. "And Jabez called on the God of Israel" (1 Chronicles 4:10). He did not call on his potential. He did not call on his network. He did not call on his strategy. He called on the God of Israel. That phrase matters because it points to covenant. It points to the God who made promises to Abraham, Isaac, and Jacob. The God who delivers, provides, speaks, and sustains.

Prayer is the place where weakness meets omnipotence.

Prayer is not decorative spirituality. It is not what we do after trying everything else. It is the place where a leader admits, I cannot do this in my own strength, but I know the God who can. For a planter, this is everything. Your greatest advantage is not your experience, your education, or your personality. Your greatest advantage is access. You have access to God.

Prayer is not preparation for the work; prayer is the work. If you ever lose that conviction, you will start to substitute activity for power. And activity without power eventually produces exhaustion.

The Boldness of the Request

Then Jabez prays something that feels almost uncomfortable. "Oh that thou wouldest bless me indeed" (1 Chronicles 4:10). At first glance, that sounds self-focused. Many leaders instinctively pull back from praying like that. They have been taught to avoid selfish ambition, to guard against pride, and to be cautious about asking God for more. So they pray safe prayers. Measured prayers. Survival prayers.

But Jabez prayed something different.

The Hebrew structure intensifies the request. It carries the sense of "bless me greatly" or "bless me abundantly." The word translated "bless" here is *barak*. It does not simply mean material increase. It means empowerment, favor, and divine enablement. When Jabez asked for blessing, he was not asking for comfort. He was asking for capacity.

That distinction is critical for planters.

A pioneer does not pray for blessing because they want an easier life. They pray for blessing because the assignment requires more strength, wisdom, and influence than they naturally possess. You need favor that opens doors you cannot open yourself. You need wisdom beyond your experience. You need courage when momentum dips, and questions rise.

A. W. Tozer challenged believers with these words: "We are too easily satisfied with a little blessing."[5] Scripture teaches that blessing becomes dangerous only when it replaces dependence. Moses warned Israel that prosperity could cause them to forget the Lord (Deuteronomy 8:11-14). That is why Jabez's prayer is so instructive. He was not asking to become self-sufficient. He was asking to become more effective in what God had called him to do.

Faith-filled expectation is not arrogance. It is alignment with God's power.

Enlarge My Territory

Jabez continues. "And enlarge my coast" (1 Chronicles 4:10). The word "coast" refers to boundaries, territory, or sphere of influence. In the ancient world, territory meant responsibility. It meant stewardship. It meant people. Jabez was not asking for more land so he could possess more. He was asking for more responsibility so he could steward more.

What does it look like for a planter to pray, "Enlarge my territory"? It might sound like this. God, send more people than I can currently handle, and help me grow into the leader who can shepherd them. Give us more Bible studies than we currently have teachers, and help us raise up laborers. Expand our reach beyond our comfort, and give us the systems to support it. Those are dangerous prayers. They require change, growth, and deeper dependence. They position you for divine activity.

How many churches remain small not because God refused to move, but because no one dared to ask Him for more?

F. B. Meyer once wrote, "The tragedy of life is not unanswered prayer, but unoffered prayer."[6] That is a sobering thought. How much ministry potential remains unrealized, not because God said no, but because no one asked?

But notice what Jabez prays next. "That thine hand might be with me" (1 Chronicles 4:10). He does not just ask for expansion. He asks for presence. That is the balance. Expansion without God leads to exhaustion. Growth without God leads to chaos. Influence without God leads to pride. Planters do not need bigger churches nearly as much as they need a stronger sense of God's presence.

Finally, Jabez prays. "That thou wouldest keep me from evil, that it may not grieve me" (1 Chronicles 4:10). He understood that success introduces new risks. Growth creates new pressures. Influence exposes new vulnerabilities. So he asked God not just to bless him but to guard him. Growth tests character as much as hardship does. A struggling season tests endurance. A successful season tests humility.

And then the text delivers one of the simplest and most powerful statements in Scripture. "And God granted him that which he requested" (1 Chronicles 4:10). God answered. Not because Jabez was perfect. Not because his circumstances were ideal. But because he prayed. Because he believed. Because he asked.

When God Says Yes

That sentence is both inspiring and searching. It is inspiring because it reminds us that God still answers prayer. He is not distant. He is not indifferent. He is not reluctant to move on behalf of those who call on Him. The same God who heard Jabez still hears the prayers of planters today.

But it is also searching. It forces us to ask a deeper question. Why did God trust Jabez with that kind of answer? The text does not begin with his request. It begins with his character. "And Jabez was more honourable than his brethren" (1 Chronicles 4:9). Before expansion, there was substance. Before blessing, there was weight. Before influence, there was integrity.

That order matters. God is not only interested in answering your prayer. He is interested in shaping your life.

God trusts greater influence to people more interested in character than image.

Planters often focus on visible growth. Attendance. Buildings. Momentum. Reach. Those things matter. They are part of the assignment. But what God does in you will always matter more than what God does through you. Because what God does through you can grow faster than your character develops. And when that happens, pressure exposes weakness.

Here is the leadership truth. God expands ministry in proportion to the leader's capacity to carry it. If capacity is lacking, expansion becomes unsustainable. And God loves you too much to give you something that will ultimately harm you.

Dallas Willard captured this reality when he wrote that the greatest issue facing the church is whether those identified as Christians will become genuine disciples.[7] The same is true for planters. The greatest issue is not whether you can gather a crowd. It is whether you can become the kind of disciple who can lead that crowd well. Your ministry should not outgrow your maturity. That does not mean you wait until you feel ready. You never will. It means you commit to growing as fast as the assignment grows.

The Rhythms That Sustain

Formation does not happen accidentally. It happens intentionally. Every planter must build rhythms that nurture spiritual depth while carrying leadership responsibility. That includes daily time with God that is not sermon preparation. Honest self-evaluation. Accountability relationships with voices that speak truth. Margin for rest and reflection. Ongoing development through reading and learning.

You cannot lead people to places you are not personally going. Your walk with God must exist apart from your role as a preacher. Burnout is not a badge of honor. It is often a warning sign of imbalance. And isolation is dangerous for leaders. You need voices in your life who can speak truth, not just encouragement.

Bill Hybels once observed, "The leader's highest task is to take responsibility for his or her own spiritual formation."[8] These rhythms are not optional. They are foundational. The sustainability of your ministry is directly tied to the health of your soul.

Carrying the Weight

There is a story often told about the construction of the Brooklyn Bridge in the late 1800s. John Roebling, the engineer who designed it, believed it could be built when others said it was impossible. During construction, Roebling was injured, and his son Washington took over. Then tragedy struck again. Washington became severely ill and was left largely paralyzed.

The project could have ended there. But it did not. Unable to move or speak normally, Washington Roebling continued to lead the construction by tapping instructions to his wife, Emily, who communicated them to the engineers. For over a decade, the bridge was built under pressure, criticism, and limitation. But it stood. And when it was finished, it became one of the most remarkable engineering achievements of its time.

The bridge could not be built without the design. But it also could not be built without the endurance to carry the weight of the process. Church planting is the same. Vision is essential. Endurance is required. Calling is critical. Character maintains it.

From Asking to Becoming

By now, the progression should be clear. Faith leads you to believe. Prayer leads you to ask. Formation determines what you can sustain. Jabez prayed a bold prayer, and God answered. But the story begins with who he was. "More honourable than his brethren" (1 Chronicles 4:9). That is not a detail. That is the foundation.

It is one thing to ask for blessing. It is another thing to become someone God can trust with it.

God does not just answer prayers. He entrusts people. He entrusts His work to those who are becoming the kind of leaders who can carry it. If God is willing to bless, if God is willing to expand, if God responds to bold, faith-filled prayer, then the question remains. What kind of life does He bless?

Jesus answers that question, not in a strategy session, but in a sermon. On a hillside. He describes the kind of person who can live under the blessing of God. Not just pray for it. Sustain it. Because the future of your ministry will not only be determined by what you ask God to do. It will be determined by who you are becoming as He does it.

So pray like Evan Roberts. Four words if that is all you have. Bend me, O Lord. Ask for blessing indeed. Ask for enlarged territory. Ask for His hand upon you. Ask for protection from evil. And then roll up your sleeves and become the kind of leader who can carry the answer.

Heaven is waiting for someone to ask.

Discussion & Application

Use these questions for personal reflection or group discussion.

1. Jabez was described as "more honourable than his brethren" (1 Chronicles 4:9) before his prayer was answered. What does that reveal about the relationship between character and blessing in ministry, and which matters more to you right now?

2. Where in your current season are you asking God for expansion, but He may be inviting you into deeper formation first? What practical step will you take this week to ensure your spiritual life grows at the pace of your ministry?

3. Many believers feel uncomfortable asking God for blessing or expansion. What lies or false assumptions about humility might be keeping you from praying bold, faith-filled prayers like Jabez?

4. Hebrews 10:35 warns believers not to "cast away confidence." What specific situations in your church plant most threaten your spiritual confidence, and what practices will help you guard against discouragement?

5. In what ways can success become more dangerous than struggle in ministry, and how does Jabez's prayer for protection model a safeguard? What rhythms do you need to establish or strengthen to ensure long-term sustainability in your calling?

Chapter Eight

The Life God Blesses

A pastor once sat at his kitchen table, staring down at a Sonic foot-long chili cheese dog. It had been a long day. Ministry responsibilities had stacked up, conversations had drained him, and somewhere along the way, he had skipped a proper meal. Now, finally, he had a few quiet minutes to himself.

He unwrapped the foil, looked at what was in front of him, and paused. Then a thought came to him, unexpected, almost humorous, but strangely weighty: Can God bless a chili cheese dog? At first, the question felt trivial. Almost silly. But the longer he sat there, the more it pressed on him. Not because of the food itself, but because of what it represented.

We have all prayed those kinds of prayers. "Lord, bless this." "Lord, bless my work." "Lord, bless this ministry." "Lord, bless this church plant." But in that quiet moment, something deeper surfaced.

Not everything is blessable.

That realization shifts the entire conversation. It moves us beyond asking for God's blessing and forces us to consider whether our lives are aligned in a way that God can actually bless. In the previous chapter, we explored the prayer of Jabez: "Oh that thou wouldest bless me indeed" (1 Chronicles 4:10). It is a bold prayer. A faith-filled prayer. But every church planter must wrestle with a tension that sits just beneath it.

It is one thing to ask for blessing. It is another thing to live a life God can bless.

God's blessing is not merely about what He does for us. It is about what He can entrust to us. Deuteronomy 28 makes the order unmistakably clear: "And it shall come to pass, if thou shalt hearken diligently unto the voice of the Lord thy God, to observe and to do all his commandments which I command thee this day, that the Lord thy God will set thee on high above all nations of the earth: And all these blessings shall come on thee, and overtake thee, if thou shalt hearken unto the voice of the Lord thy God" (Deuteronomy 28:1–2). Obedience comes first. Blessing follows.

We often want to reverse that order. We ask for blessing and hope obedience will catch up later. But God forms the person before He releases the promise. He develops the vessel before He pours into it. Because God's blessing is not a reward for ambition. It is the fruit of alignment. And nowhere is that more important than in church planting.

A church planter can have the right strategy, the right location, and the right team. But if the inner life of the leader is not aligned with the heart of God, the work will eventually reflect that misalignment. God does not simply bless activity. He blesses lives that are surrendered, obedient, and positioned under His authority. The question is not whether God wants to bless. The question is whether we have built a life that can carry what He wants to give.

The Spirit Behind the Strategy

Church-planting conversations often center on strategy. Where will you launch? Who will be on your team? What is your timeline? What systems will you build? How will you fund it? All of those questions matter. They deserve careful thought. But none of them are primary. Because at the end of the day, the church you plant will not merely reflect your strategy.

It will reflect your spirit.

Numbers 11 gives us a powerful window into how God works in leadership. The Lord said concerning Moses, "I will take of the spirit which is upon thee, and will put it upon them" (Numbers 11:17). God did not simply assign responsibility to the seventy elders. He shared Moses' spirit with them. That is still how leadership works. What is in the leader gets reproduced in the people.[1]

If the leader carries faith, the church will grow in faith. If the leader carries anxiety, the church will feel it. If the leader walks in humility, the culture will reflect it. If the leader operates in pride or insecurity, it will eventually surface. Spirit is transferable, not because you announce it, but because you live it.

You will not reproduce what you teach. You will reproduce who you are.

That truth is both encouraging and sobering. It is encouraging because personal growth creates collective growth. But it is sobering because unresolved issues do not stay hidden forever. They eventually surface in culture, in relationships, and in leadership decisions that seem to come from nowhere but have actually been forming for a long time.

That is why Proverbs 4:23 instructs us so clearly: "Keep thy heart with all diligence; for out of it are the issues of life." Everything flows from the heart. Your leadership. Your decisions. Your church culture. Church planting is not just about reaching a city. It is about stewarding a spirit.

Jesus Redefines the Blessed Life

This is exactly why Jesus begins His most famous sermon the way He does. "And seeing the multitudes, he went up into a mountain: and when he was set, his disciples came unto him: And he opened his mouth, and taught them" (Matthew 5:1–2). This is not casual instruction. This is kingdom definition. Jesus is about to redefine what it means to be blessed.

"Blessed are the poor in spirit: for theirs is the kingdom of heaven" (Matthew 5:3). The word "blessed" here does not simply mean happy. It means approved by God. Aligned with God. Living under His favor. And Jesus begins not with strength but with humility.

Poverty of Spirit

To be "poor in spirit" is not to have low self-esteem. It is to have accurate awareness. It is to recognize that apart from God, we have nothing, no strength, no wisdom, no ability that can maintain what He is calling us to do. It is complete dependence. And Jesus says that is where the Kingdom begins.[2]

One of the greatest dangers in church planting is not weakness. It is strength. It is competence. It is the ability to communicate well, organize effectively, and lead confidently. Those are gifts from God, but they can quietly become substitutes for dependence on God. The more capable you are, the easier it is to rely on your experience, your instincts, your preparation. And without realizing it, you begin building something for God without truly depending on God.

God does not bless self-sufficiency. He blesses surrender.

Tender Hearts and Submitted Strength

Jesus continues: "Blessed are they that mourn: for they shall be comforted" (Matthew 5:4). This is not casual sadness. This is a deep sensitivity to sin, brokenness, and the condition of both the human heart and the world around us. Church planters who lose the ability to mourn will eventually lose the ability to minister effectively. They may still preach well. They may still organize efficiently. But something vital will be missing.

When a leader stops mourning over sin, stops grieving over lost people, stops feeling the weight of broken lives, ministry shifts from compassion to performance. It becomes something you do instead of something you carry. A tender heart keeps ministry alive. People can sense authenticity. They recognize when a pastor is not just leading a church, but loving people.

Ministry without a tender heart becomes mechanical.

"Blessed are the meek: for they shall inherit the earth" (Matthew 5:5). Meekness is one of the most misunderstood qualities in leadership. It is often mistaken for weakness or passivity. But meekness is strength under control, power that has been surrendered to God. The word Jesus uses was often applied to a trained animal, something that still possessed great strength but had learned to operate under authority.[3]

In church planting, meekness is not optional. You will be misunderstood. You will be criticized. You will encounter situations where you can assert yourself or prove your point. Meekness chooses restraint. It chooses wisdom over reaction. It chooses long-term fruit over short-term satisfaction.

Your calling is not sustained by your image. It is sustained by your obedience.

Hunger, Mercy, and Purity

"Blessed are they which do hunger and thirst after righteousness: for they shall be filled" (Matthew 5:6). Hunger is a powerful force. It drives decisions, shapes priorities, and determines direction. Jesus says the blessed life is marked by a deep craving, not for success, not for recognition, not for growth metrics, but for righteousness. What you hunger for determines who you become.

If your hunger is for success, you may build something visible. If your hunger is for approval, you may build something impressive. But if your hunger is for righteousness, you will build something that lasts. Because God fills what aligns with His heart. Your spiritual appetite will determine your leadership altitude. Church planters must guard their appetite because the demands of ministry can easily shift what they crave.

"Blessed are the merciful: for they shall obtain mercy" (Matthew 5:7). Mercy is not just something you feel. It is something you extend. It is compassion in motion. In a church plant, you will meet people at their worst: broken, confused, inconsistent, and sometimes frustrating. People who do not respond the way you hoped. People who require more patience than you expected to give.

Mercy chooses to stay patient when it would be easier to withdraw. It chooses to believe the best when it would be easier to assume the worst. It chooses to walk with people rather than write them off. Because mercy is not about what people deserve. It is about reflecting the heart of God.

"Blessed are the pure in heart: for they shall see God" (Matthew 5:8). Purity of heart is not about perfection. It is about focus, a life that is not divided by competing motives. In ministry, it is possible to serve out of a desire for validation or to lead out of a need for identity. But purity brings alignment. It asks a simple question: Why am I doing this? A pure heart sees what a divided heart cannot.

"Blessed are the peacemakers: for they shall be called the children of God" (Matthew 5:9). Peacemakers are not passive. They are intentional. They step into conflict and work to bring resolution. Wherever people gather, differences will surface.

Miscommunication will happen. Expectations will clash. And in those moments, the leader sets the tone. Peacemakers do not avoid conflict. They engage it with wisdom, humility, and a desire for restoration. Because peace is not the absence of conflict. It is the presence of Christ in the middle of it.

Jesus concludes with a reality every church planter will eventually face: "Blessed are they which are persecuted for righteousness' sake: for theirs is the kingdom of heaven" (Matthew 5:10). Living differently creates pressure. Leading with conviction invites resistance. Standing for truth will not always be applauded. But Jesus reframes that resistance. He calls it blessed. Because sometimes opposition is not a sign that something is wrong. Sometimes it is evidence of forward movement.

Friction is not always failure. Sometimes it is confirmation.

When Your Spirit Becomes the Culture

There comes a moment in every church plant when something subtle but truly significant happens. What began as vision starts becoming culture. What was once intentional becomes instinctive. And what you have been carrying internally begins to show up externally in the people you are leading. It is one of the most powerful dynamics in ministry.

You begin to notice it in conversations. In attitudes. In how people respond to pressure and opportunity. And if you pay attention, you will recognize something both powerful and sobering: the culture you are leading is becoming the spirit you carry. Not because you taught it in a lesson. Not because you wrote it in a handbook. But because you lived it.

Over time, the tone of your spirit becomes the tone of the church. If you carry peace, people feel it. If you carry anxiety, people absorb it. If you carry joy, it spreads. If you carry frustration, it leaks. People may hear what you say. But they will become what you are.

This is why Numbers 11 remains so instructive. God said, "I will take of the spirit which is upon thee, and will put it upon them" (Numbers 11:17). God did not multiply Moses' systems. He multiplied his spirit. And that is still how the Kingdom works.

This leads to a leadership reality that cannot be avoided: you cannot impart what you do not possess. You cannot lead people into a place you have not gone. You cannot reproduce a spirit you have not cultivated. That is why internal health is not optional. It is essential. Because eventually, your private life will become public fruit.

Jesus said, "A good man out of the good treasure of his heart bringeth forth that which is good" (Luke 6:45). What is stored internally will eventually be expressed externally.

Ministry does not hide who you are. It reveals who you are. And over time, it multiplies it.

Guarding the Well

So how does a church planter nurture the kind of life God can bless? It does not happen accidentally. It happens intentionally. It happens in daily, unseen moments that no one applauds or measures. Jesus modeled this consistently. In the middle of growing crowds and increasing demands, Scripture tells us, "And in the morning, rising up a great while before day, he went out, and departed into a solitary place, and there prayed" (Mark 1:35).

What is built publicly must be sustained privately.

Church planters must learn this early. You do not build spiritual strength in moments of crisis. You reveal it. What you have developed in private is what you will draw from in public. In the early stages of a church plant, your schedule will fill faster than you expect. People will need your attention. Decisions will demand your energy. Opportunities will compete for your time. And in the middle of all of that, it becomes dangerously easy to neglect the very thing that nourishes everything else: your relationship with God.

Neglecting your inner life does not simplify ministry. It complicates it. When connection weakens, clarity fades. When clarity fades, pressure increases. When pressure increases, fatigue follows. And when fatigue sets in, the spirit begins to erode. That is why guarding your inner life is not selfish. It is stewardship. You are protecting the source from which everything flows.

Paul described this honestly when he wrote, "We are troubled on every side, yet not distressed; we are perplexed, but not in despair" (2 Corinthians 4:8). That is the language of a leader who has learned to maintain the right spirit. Pressure without collapse. Questions without quitting. Because the strength is not coming from circumstances. It is coming from connection.

You can only lead people as far as your private walk with God will carry you.

The Danger of Drift

One of the greatest threats to a church planter is not failure. It is drift. Hebrews warns us, "Therefore we ought to give the more earnest heed to the things which we have heard, lest at any time we should let them slip" (Hebrews 2:1). Drift is subtle. It does not happen all at once. Prayer becomes shorter. Scripture becomes occasional. Conviction becomes flexible. Focus becomes divided. And over time, what once burned brightly begins to fade quietly.[4]

No one notices at first. But eventually, everyone feels it. Because spirit is transferable. Jesus addressed this directly when He spoke to the church at Ephesus: "Nevertheless I have somewhat against thee, because thou hast left thy first love" (Revelation 2:4). Notice, He did not say they lost it. He said they left it. It was not taken from them. It was gradually set aside.

But the solution was just as clear: "Remember therefore from whence thou art fallen, and repent, and do the first works" (Revelation 2:5). Return. Realign. Reconnect. Church planters must build rhythms that bring them back to first things, not occasionally, but consistently. Because what you return to determines what you sustain.

The Village and the Well

There was once a village that depended entirely on a single well. For generations, that well provided everything the people needed: water for drinking, for cooking, for sustaining life. As long as the well was full, the village thrived. Over time, the village grew. People became busy. Buildings expanded. Life became more complex. And slowly, almost without noticing, they stopped paying attention to the well.

They assumed it would always be there. Always be full. Always be enough. Until one day someone lowered the bucket, and it came back empty. Panic set in. Because everything they had built depended on a source they had neglected. And in that moment, they realized something too late: you cannot neglect the source and expect continued supply.

Church planter, your spirit is that well. Your relationship with God is that source. And everything you are building depends on it.

That pastor sitting at his kitchen table eventually bowed his head to pray. But his prayer had changed. It was no longer just, "Lord, bless this." It became, "Lord, shape me into someone You can bless." That is where real ministry begins. Not with asking but with becoming. Because before God builds something through you, He will build something in you.

The prayer of Jabez teaches us to ask boldly. The Beatitudes teach us the kind of life God blesses. But maintaining that life requires daily connection to the source. Because the church is not ultimately built by strategy. It is enabled by the Spirit of God and the Word of God.

And while your relationship with God is foundational, there is another relationship that will either strengthen or strain everything you are building. It is the relationship closest to you. It is the one that sees you when the crowds are gone, and the platform is empty. It is the relationship that carries the weight of your calling right alongside you.

Your family. And that is where we now turn.

Discussion & Application

Use these questions for personal reflection or group discussion.

1. The chapter opens with the question "Can God bless a chili cheese dog?" and moves toward the deeper issue of whether our lives are positioned for blessing. In what areas of your leadership are you asking God for blessing without first examining whether your life is aligned in a way He can bless?

2. Numbers 11:17 reveals that God multiplied Moses' spirit, not his strategy, into the seventy elders. What specific qualities of your spirit are currently being reproduced in the people you lead, and are those the qualities you want defining your church's culture?

3. Jesus begins the Beatitudes with "Blessed are the poor in spirit." How does competence and natural gifting become a subtle barrier to genuine dependence on God in your ministry, and what practices help you stay anchored in spiritual poverty?

4. The chapter warns that drift, not failure, is the greatest threat to a church planter's spiritual life. What early warning signs of drift have you noticed in your own journey, and what specific rhythms could you build to prevent your "well" from running dry?

5. The Beatitudes describe a portrait of humility, tenderness, meekness, hunger, mercy, purity, and peacemaking. Which of these qualities feels most underdeveloped in your current leadership, and what would it look like to intentionally cultivate it over the next ninety days?

Chapter Nine

The First Church You Plant

H is life could not have been going any better. He was the most sought-after evange-list in his denomination. If you wanted him to preach at your church, you got in line and waited. Four years, minimum. Invitations poured in. Doors opened effortlessly. His ministry was accelerating like a rocket.

And then the phone rang.

Every invitation that blessed his ministry pulled him further from his family. But he and his wife had found a rhythm that worked. Two weeks on the road. Two weeks at home. It was not perfect, but it was sustainable. His marriage was strong. His teenage son was thriving in school. Life felt balanced.

On the other end of the phone was his wife. The conversation was short, but it carried weight. Their sixteen-year-old son had crossed a line. Defiant. Disrespectful. Immovable. The kind of moment that reveals cracks beneath the surface. Then she said three words that changed everything. "I need you."

He did not hesitate. He canceled the remainder of his meetings and drove home immedi-ately. What he did not know was that his son was listening from the next room. The boy was watching. Testing. Waiting to see what his father would do.

Within days, a "For Sale" sign stood in the front yard. The evangelist accepted a pas-torate at a small church in another state. Then came the unthinkable. He canceled every scheduled meeting for the next four years. That decision cost him dearly. When he eventually returned to evangelism, the landscape had changed. New leaders had risen. Old connections had faded. In many ways, his ministry never fully recovered.

But his son did.

Years later, that teenage boy, James Dobson, would go on to found Focus on the Family, a ministry currently heard on about two thousand radio stations worldwide, reaching millions of people.[1] Dr. Dobson himself later reflected that his father's decision was a pivotal moment. His father put him ahead of his profession and saw that he could lose his son during those critical years. He was not about to let that happen.

When asked about his success, Dr. Dobson pointed first to Jesus Christ, and then to one man, his father, James Dobson Sr. He said Focus on the Family was a product of his father's ministry, and especially of his prayer life. A man who chose his family over his platform. A man who understood a truth every church planter must embrace.

You cannot build God's church while neglecting the first church He gave you, which is your home.

The Small Church You Pastor First

Scripture is not silent on this issue. Paul writes that a leader must be "one that ruleth well his own house, having his children in subjection with all gravity" (1 Timothy 3:4). Then he continues, "For if a man know not how to rule his own house, how shall he take care of the church of God?" (1 Timothy 3:5). That is not a suggestion. That is a qualification. Before God entrusts you with His church, He examines how you steward your home.

In the fourth century, John Chrysostom used a phrase that still ought to arrest every church planter. He called the home, newly created in the marriage covenant, "the small church."[2] When a husband and wife exchange vows, he argued, they are anointed by the Spirit of God to function as the priesthood of this church-in-miniature. They are the redeemed Adam and Eve, tasked with building a particular place of worship on planet Earth. In that tiny sanctuary, prayers are prayed, hands are raised to heaven instead of against each other, and the foundations of discipleship are laid.

Chrysostom believed this little home church was a microcosm of Eden itself, the place where people learn again to walk with God "in the cool of the day" (Genesis 3:8). In the Eastern Orthodox marriage service, there is a beautiful crowning ritual. The priest places wreaths made of garland, orange blossoms, or myrtle leaves on the heads of the bride and groom, tied together with a white ribbon signifying purity and unity. It is a coronation. The husband and wife are now ruling together as king and queen of a new domain. But those crowns are not ornamental. They mirror the crowns of the martyrs in Revelation 2:10. The couple has been empowered from on high to lay their lives down for each other.

That is the calling. Not consciously uncoupling when things get difficult. Not treating the home as optional infrastructure. But living into the same kind of covenant Jesus shares with His bride, the church. A communion sealed in blood. A union enlivened by a broken body. If you are a church planter, the first sanctuary God ever gave you to pastor has a front door, a kitchen table, and a last name on the mailbox. Before you ever shepherd anyone else, you are pastoring that small church.

The first sanctuary God ever gave you to pastor has a front door, a kitchen table, and a last name on the mailbox.

George Santayana called the family one of nature's masterpieces.[3] That is exactly what your home is supposed to be. Not a burden. Not an obstacle to your anointing. A masterpiece. Daniel Grothe writes that the holy vocation of matrimony is to learn how to serve another who sees the world differently.[4] That is ministry. That is discipleship. That is church planting at the most intimate level imaginable. Every morning, you get to practice servant leadership on the two or three people who know you best. If you cannot serve them, a platform will only magnify what you lack.

Mother Teresa is often quoted as saying, "If you want to change the world, go home and love your family."[5] The woman who picked dying men out of Calcutta gutters said world change begins at the kitchen table. Heaven uses the same rhythm. As the family goes, so goes the church. If that is true of any household in your congregation, it is doubly true of yours. The leader's family is not a footnote to the mission. It is the first evidence of the mission.

The way you lead your family will inevitably bleed into the way you lead the church. This is not about perfection. It is about priority. No marriage is perfect. Every home has stress, misunderstandings, and growing pains. But Scripture calls us to something deeper than perfection. It calls us to alignment. God has never asked anyone to sacrifice their marriage on the altar of ministry. Not once. Not ever. Your marriage is not in competition with your ministry. Your children are not distractions from your calling. They are part of your calling.

What if the greatest testimony of your ministry is not the size of your church but the strength of your home? What if your children loving God is a greater miracle than a packed sanctuary? What if your marriage thriving is your most powerful sermon? The metrics of ministry are often external. Attendance. Giving. Growth. But the metrics that matter most to God are deeply personal. Peace in your home. Joy in your marriage. Connection with your children. Those are not side projects. They are central to your calling.

Be a Friend: Time Is Love Spelled Out

Charles Francis Adams was an important man, a prominent statesman, and the United States Ambassador to Great Britain under the Lincoln administration. One day, he took his young son fishing. That evening, he made a brief entry in his diary. "Went fishing with my son. A day wasted." But his son, Brooks Adams, also kept a diary. And on that same day, the boy wrote, "Went fishing with my father. The most glorious day of my life."[6]

Same day. Same moment. Two completely different interpretations. One saw an interruption. The other received a memory that would last a lifetime. That is the reality every church planter must navigate. What you see as an interruption, your children experience as an invitation. What you dismiss as a small moment, they remember as a defining one. Your children are writing their own version of that story right now. Every dinner you miss. Every school activity you skip. Every moment you are physically present but emotionally absent. They are taking notes.

In our home, we have tried to build rhythms that create space for connection. Every quarter, I take each of my boys on what we call "Daddy Day Out." It is nothing extravagant. One likes to hike. Another is a foodie. The youngest is happy to do just about anything. There is no agenda. No teaching outline. No hidden sermon. The goal is simple. Be together. My wife and I also schedule a quarterly date night. Not complicated. But intentional. You do not drift into connection. You design for it. Children spell love T-I-M-E.

God has always emphasized presence in the family. Deuteronomy 6:6–7 says, "And these words, which I command thee this day, shall be in thine heart: And thou shalt teach them diligently unto thy children, and shalt talk of them when thou sittest in thine house, and when thou walkest by the way, and when thou liest down, and when thou risest up." Notice the rhythm. Sitting. Walking. Lying down. Rising up. This is not about scheduling one big spiritual moment a week. It is about weaving your life into theirs. Presence is not an event. It is a lifestyle.

If you do not intentionally schedule time with your family, your ministry will schedule it out of existence. There will always be another meeting. Another call. Another crisis. But your children will not always be under your roof. And your spouse will not always wait patiently for "when things slow down." Because they never will.

What you call a sacrifice for ministry, your family may experience as abandonment.

Be a Fan: Speak Life Relentlessly

If being a friend is about your presence, being a fan is about your voice. And your words carry more weight in your home than anywhere else. Proverbs 18:21 says, "Death and life are in the power of the tongue: and they that love it shall eat the fruit thereof." Your words will either build your family up or slowly tear them down.

The Power of a Father's Voice

There is a story about a major league baseball player who was once asked how he made it to the highest level of his sport. He said, "Almost every day, my dad would tell me, 'Son, if you keep throwing like that, one day you'll be a major leaguer.'" In the same conversation, an inmate listening nearby spoke up. He said, "That's interesting. My dad told me almost every day that I'd end up in jail." And he did. Two fathers. Two voices. Two outcomes.

Your words over your family should echo what God has already spoken. When you speak life over your children and your spouse, you are aligning your home with the voice of heaven. Speak Philippians 4:13 over them. "I can do all things through Christ which strengtheneth me." Speak Jeremiah 29:11 over them. "For I know the thoughts that I think toward you, saith the Lord, thoughts of peace, and not of evil, to give you an expected end." Your words can become the atmosphere your family breathes.

Abigail and the King Inside David

One of the most powerful examples of speaking life appears in 1 Samuel 25. David is in a dangerous place emotionally, spiritually, and mentally. He has been dishonored by a wealthy man named Nabal and is riding toward violence. He is moments away from making a decision that would stain his future with innocent blood. Then Abigail steps in. She does not just stop him. She speaks to him. She tells him that the Lord will certainly make a lasting dynasty for him because he fights the Lord's battles (1 Samuel 25:28–30).

She saw what he could not see about himself in that moment. She spoke to the king in David before the crown was ever on his head. She called out his future in the middle of his frustration. She did not lecture him about his anger. She did not criticize his decision. She spoke to the destiny inside him that was temporarily buried under offense. And something in David responded. The king stood up.

Your spouse and children need someone who can call out who they are becoming, not just correct who they are today.

Your spouse and your children need someone who can see beyond the moment they are in. They need someone who can call out who they are becoming, not just correct who they are today. Choose wisely what you speak over the people who share your dinner table and your last name.

A Mother's Arms Around the World

During World War II, a sailor named Elgin Staples survived two devastating shipwrecks in the Battle of Savo Island. Both times, he was thrown into the Pacific Ocean. Both times, an inflatable life belt kept him afloat until rescue arrived. When he returned home to Akron, Ohio, he showed the belt to his mother, Vera. She immediately recognized it. She had inspected it. Stamped it. Approved it. The belt bore her personal inspection number from the Firestone Tire and Rubber Company. The very device that saved her son's life, twice, had passed through his own mother's hands. Elgin later said wearing that belt felt like having his mother's arms around him.

That is what your words can be for your family. A life-preserving force. A steadying presence. A reminder that someone believes in them even when they cannot believe in themselves.

Be a Forgiver: Release What You Cannot Repair

Every family, no matter how healthy, will experience hurt. Misunderstandings will happen. Harsh words will be spoken. Disappointment will surface. And sometimes deep wounds will appear where you least expect them. The question is not whether your family will need forgiveness. The question is whether your home will be a place where forgiveness flows freely.

In Matthew 18, Peter asks, "Lord, how oft shall my brother sin against me, and I forgive him? till seven times?" Jesus responds, "I say not unto thee, Until seven times: but, Until seventy times seven" (Matthew 18:21–22). In other words, you do not keep score. You keep forgiving. Jesus then tells the parable of the unforgiving servant, a man forgiven an enormous, unpayable debt who then refuses to forgive a fellow servant who owes him far less. The master's response is severe. The message is unmistakable. Forgiven people forgive people.

Let me be clear about what forgiveness is and what it is not. Forgiveness is not saying the offense was no big deal. Forgiveness is not pretending everything is fine. And forgiveness does not always mean restoring the relationship to its previous form. Consider Joseph's wisdom in his dealings with his brothers in Genesis 42–45. He forgave them fully but tested their character before restoring the relationship. Forgiveness is refusing to collect a debt that cannot be repaid.

Lewis Smedes said it memorably. "To forgive is to set a prisoner free and discover that the prisoner was you."[7] Church planters carry enormous pressure. And pressure has a way of leaking. If you are not careful, your family becomes the place where your frustrations are expressed most freely. That is why forgiveness must be a constant rhythm in your home. Not just receiving it, but extending it.

Jesus reinforces this in Matthew 6:14–15. "For if ye forgive men their trespasses, your heavenly Father will also forgive you: But if ye forgive not men their trespasses, neither will your Father forgive your trespasses." This is not optional. It is foundational. Forgiveness is not a punishment imposed on the offended. It is a privilege offered to the wounded. It sets the prisoner free, and the prisoner is often you. A home without forgiveness becomes a place where love slowly suffocates.

What Your Family is Worth

In 1918, a doctor gave a professional heavyweight boxer named Billy Miske devastating news. He had Bright's disease, a severe kidney condition, and would likely not live to see thirty. The recommendation was clear. Stop fighting. But Billy had a family. And he had debt. So he kept stepping into the ring. He fought thirty more times after his diagnosis, including bouts against Jack Dempsey. Every punch pushed his fragile body closer to collapse.

As Christmas 1923 approached, Billy's body was failing. Training was nearly impossible. But he wanted one last Christmas for his wife and three children. Not a quiet one. A full one. A joyful one. So he asked his manager for one final fight. The manager resisted. "Billy, in your condition, you could get killed." Billy replied, "What's the difference? It's better than waiting for it in a rocking chair."

The fight lasted four rounds. The emaciated, deathly ill Billy Miske knocked his opponent out. He walked away with twenty-four hundred dollars. That Christmas morning, his children woke to a house filled with gifts. A toy train circled the room. His wife received the piano she had always dreamed of. Laughter filled every corner. The day after Christmas, Billy called his trainer and said, "Come get me. I'm dying." Shortly after, he passed away at twenty-nine. But he left his family with something that would outlive him. A memory. A legacy. A demonstration of love that cost him everything.

Never bet against a father determined to sacrifice for his family. You may never step into a boxing ring. But you will face moments just as defining. Moments where your decisions will shape your family's future. The question you must answer is this. What is your family worth to you? Not in theory. Not in sermons. Not in conversations at pastors' conferences. But in decisions. Your spouse needs more than your promises. They need your presence. Your children do not just need your instruction. They need your investment.

Your family is not competing with your calling. They are confirming it.

A Promise Worth Keeping

Kent Hughes tells the story of Robertson McQuilkin, the former president of Columbia International University.[8] When his wife Muriel was diagnosed with Alzheimer's, Mc-

Quilkin faced a decision. Continue leading a thriving institution or step away to care for his wife full-time. He chose his wife. In his resignation letter, he wrote words every church planter should carry. "This decision was made, in a way, forty-two years ago when I promised to care for her 'in sickness and in health, till death do us part.' She has cared for me fully all these years. If I cared for her for the next forty years I would not be out of debt. Duty, however, can be grim and stoic. But there is more. I love Muriel. I do not have to care for her. I get to."

That is not obligation. That is covenant. And covenant always costs something.

From Preparation to Launch

This chapter closes Part 2 of this book, the preparation phase. We have talked about calling. We have talked about character. We have talked about submission, formation, and faith. And now we have talked about family. Because before you launch a church, God prepares a person. And while He prepares a person, He shapes a home. As we move into Part 3, everything shifts. We are going from preparation to action. From formation to function. From burden to building. The conversations ahead will be about strategy, structure, teams, and launch. But if you skip what we have covered in Part 2, Part 3 will eventually collapse under the weight of what was never built properly.

You can launch fast. But you can only last if your foundation is strong.

Do Not Plant a Church

Before we move to the practical steps of planting a church, let me speak plainly. Do not plant a church if your spouse is not fully on board. Do not plant a church without your pastor's approval. Do not plant a church if you are not proficient in teaching Home Bible Studies. Do not plant a church if your finances are a mess. Do not plant a church if you are emotionally unstable. Do not plant a church if your marriage is in trouble.

God may indeed have called you to plant a church. But if you do not handle these challenges properly, they will greatly hinder the work God wants to do through you. If your spouse is not in agreement, you may be called, but the timing is not right. Do not try to convince them of the call. Be quiet and let God speak to them. If He does, proceed. If He does not, either it is not the time or you are not called. The same can be said of your pastor.

In the formative stage of a new church, typically, the church planter and their family are the only people with experience teaching Home Bible Studies. Attempting to plant a church with disordered finances can spell disaster for you and the congregation. In the early days of a church, the largest financial contributors are often the pastor's family. The church planter often carries the church financially, not the other way around.

Church planting is emotionally challenging by nature. An emotionally unstable planter will have a very difficult time establishing a healthy church. Health attracts health. Dysfunction attracts dysfunction. Before you attempt to launch a church, get help. Seek counseling. Seek guidance. Get healthy. Make sure that you and your spouse are in love with God and each other. Ensure that your marriage is healthy and growing before attempting to replicate it in a new congregation.

Discussion & Application

Use these questions for personal reflection or group discussion.

1. James Dobson Sr. canceled four years of scheduled meetings to be present for his teenage son. What would it cost you to make a similar decision right now, and what might it produce in the long run if you did?

2. John Chrysostom called the home the "small church," where the husband and wife function as its priesthood. If you evaluated yourself as the pastor of that small church, what would your sermon, your shepherding, and your prayer life look like this week?

3. Abigail spoke to the king inside David. Who in your family needs you to speak to their future instead of only correcting their present? What specific words of life could you begin speaking over them this week?

4. The chapter defines forgiveness as "refusing to collect a debt that cannot be repaid." Is there an unresolved offense in your home that is quietly eroding trust? What would it look like to release that debt and restore the atmosphere of your family?

5. Robertson McQuilkin wrote, "I do not have to care for her. I get to." How does that distinction between duty and delight reshape the way you think about the daily sacrifices required to lead your family well while planting a church?

Part 3: The Launch

"Have not I commanded thee? Be strong and of a good courage; be not afraid, neither be thou dismayed: for the Lord thy God is with thee whithersoever thou goest" (Joshua 1:9).

"The vigorous, continual planting of new congregations is the single most crucial strategy for the numerical growth of the Body of Christ." – Tim Keller

Built to Stand Together

In Northern California, the redwoods rise like cathedrals. Some climb over three hundred feet, taller than a football field is long. Their trunks are massive. Their presence is overwhelming. Stand at the base of one, and you feel small in the best possible way. But the most fascinating thing about a redwood is not what towers above the ground. It is what hides beneath it.

Redwoods do not have deep roots.

In fact, their roots only reach about six to twelve feet into the soil. That is shockingly shallow for a tree of that size. If a redwood stood alone, it would topple under its own weight. The first strong storm would finish the job. So how in the world do they stand?

Their roots grow outward instead of downward. As they spread, they intertwine with the roots of the surrounding trees. They literally lock arms beneath the forest floor. Each tree strengthens the others. Each root system supports its neighbor. Every trunk stands tall because it is connected to something bigger than itself.

A redwood does not stand because it is strong. It stands because it is supported.[1]

That truth is not just botanical. It is spiritual. It is leadership. It is ministry. And it is the foundation of every church plant that lasts.

You Were Never Meant to Stand Alone

Church planting has a way of attracting strong people. Visionaries. Builders. Risk-takers. Sons and daughters of God who feel a divine pull toward places where nothing yet exists. That calling is sacred. But it can also be dangerous. Because if you are not careful, the very strength that qualifies you to plant a church can deceive you into believing you can build it alone.

You cannot.

No matter how gifted a church planter may be. No matter how anointed they feel. No matter how clear the vision is. If they try to stand alone, they will not last. Church planting is not sustained by individual strength. It is sustained by collective support. You don't build a church by standing tall. You build a church by staying connected.

Prayer partners become your unseen roots. Financial supporters become your stabilizing strength. A launch team becomes your interwoven support system. The strongest churches are not built on the back of one leader. They are built on the shoulders of a connected team. There is an old proverb that says, "If you want to go fast, go alone. If you want to go far, go together." Church planting is not a sprint. It is a lifelong assignment, and you will never go far without a team.[2]

Even Moses, the great deliverer of Israel, could not lead alone. When Israel battled Amalek, Moses stood on the hill with the rod of God in his hand. As long as his arms were raised, Israel prevailed. But when his arms grew weary, the battle began to turn. Victory did not waver because Moses lacked calling. It wavered because Moses lacked support. So Aaron and Hur stepped in, one on each side, and held up his hands until the sun went down.

Moses still stood. But he did not stand alone. That is the picture of church planting. You may be the one holding the rod, but you will need people holding up your arms. Every Apostolic church plant desperately needs three things: prayer support, financial support, and a launch team.

Building Your Prayer Support

Every month, I meet with a team of prayer partners. I hand them an outline of my current prayer needs. The list covers personal matters, family, physical health, finances, upcoming services, and ministry opportunities. Each partner prays for me, my family, and our ministry team on an assigned day every week. They cover every speaking engagement we have. They have covered this very book in prayer at every stage of its development.

Beyond the specific needs, I ask them to pray something deeper over my life. Pray that God will fill me with His love, wisdom, and gratitude every single day. Pray that I will humble myself under His mighty hand. Pray that He will bless me indeed, enlarge my influence, keep His hand upon me, and keep me from evil so I cause no pain. Pray that I will be poor in spirit, mourn for sin, walk in meekness, hunger and thirst for righteousness, show mercy, stay pure in heart, and make peace. Pray that I will know what God wants me to know and do what God wants me to do. Pray that I will finish well.

Each month when we gather, I update them on the answers to last month's requests. This team is integral to everything God is doing through our congregation.

Recruit a small team to faithfully cover your new church in prayer. The team does not need to be large. Ours currently sits at eight. I would rather have a small team committed to praying every day than a large team that feels no real responsibility to pray at all. There is nothing wrong with asking the masses for prayer. Just remember, when everyone is responsible, no one is responsible.

A smaller circle also lets you share more personal details. I never write anything I would not want forwarded. But I do not hand prayer lists to people who are not meeting with me consistently.[3]

Once you have at least seven prayer partners, assign each one a day of the week that fits their schedule. Then create a group text, a closed Facebook group, or some other simple way to communicate. Don't just ask for prayer. Give updates. Close the loop. Let them celebrate the answers with you. My prayer team is one of the very first groups I reach out to whenever I have a pressing need. They are the unseen roots holding everything else upright.

You are not weak because you need prayer support. You are wise because you build it.

Building Your Financial Support

It has been said that every church needs three books: the Good Book, a songbook, and a checkbook. Every successful church plant needs the Word, worship, and a way to pay the bills. Ministry and money are not in competition. They are in cooperation. Without money, you will not be able to do ministry for very long.

Hopefully, planting a church is not your first attempt at ministry. I know church planters who have started congregations with no prior experience, but I do not recommend it. Serving faithfully in a local church or as an evangelist gives you ministry experience and lays the foundation for a base of financial support. Your résumé will largely determine your resources.

If people have served alongside you, they are far more likely to support you when you launch out. If they have witnessed your love for God and others, they will believe in your ability to grow His Kingdom in a new community. If they know your spirit and your integrity, they are already invested in you. When you ask them to give, they will not view it as charity. They will view it as an investment.

People don't give to need. They give to vision.

If you are planting through an Apostolic organization, follow their guidelines for raising support. Seek the counsel of your pastor and trusted elders. Be a faithful steward of every dollar entrusted to your care. People give generously to ministries with a proven track record of excellence and a clearly communicated plan for stewarding funds wisely.[4]

Develop a launch budget. How much will facility rent cost? What about audio and video equipment, promotions, a website, graphic design, signage, and childcare? Include every line item you need to host your first service. Then break the budget into two or three phases. Phase one covers what you absolutely must have to open the doors. Phase two covers items that would greatly enhance the worship experience. Phase three is the wish list, the things it would be wonderful to have someday.

Design the budget in a clean, professional format. Present it to your pastor and trusted elders. Ask their advice on how to proceed. Your pastor and neighboring pastors may even let you present the need to their congregations. If you serve as an evangelist, present your budget to host pastors. Many will welcome the chance to invest in this new work. Don't hesitate to ask. You have not because you ask not. The funds are not for you. They are for the lost men and women in the community God is sending you to.

Above all, seek God for His provision. The church is His idea. He will always come through when you seek Him and follow His direction. In John 14:14, Jesus says, "If ye shall ask any thing in my name, I will do it." That promise is not a blank check for mansions and luxury cars. In context, Jesus is saying that whatever you need to get the job done, He will supply.

Imagine you own a massive ranch, and I come to work for you. You hand me the keys to your truck and tell me to inspect every fence post. As I am walking out the door, you say, "If you need anything, just let me know." Now imagine I call you thirty minutes later and ask for a million dollars. You would be exasperated. Your offer was not a promise for anything I want, up to half your kingdom. It was a promise to supply whatever I needed to finish the assignment. That is exactly what God promises in John 14:14.

My spiritual father, Bob McCool Sr., taught us something I have never forgotten. God will always give you what you need to get the job done. So ask. Seek. Knock. What kind of God calls a family to a city to plant a church and then refuses to provide for them? Our job is to pray and obey. His job is to answer and supply. Hudson Taylor profoundly wrote, "God's work done in God's way will never lack God's supply."[5]

Our job is to pray and obey. His job is to answer and supply.

Lastly, when people give, say thank you. There is an old saying: "Thank before you bank." That is wise advice. Thanking the donor expresses appreciation and strengthens the relationship. Often, a donor who is thanked becomes a donor who keeps giving.

Then give them a way to witness the return on their investment. Social media has made this easier than ever. Post regularly. Don't reserve updates for baptisms and Holy Ghost infillings. Take pictures of unloading the moving truck, of taking your kids to the park, and of every Bible study you teach. You don't have to photograph the people. Snap a picture of the Bible study chart and your favorite drink. When services begin, take close-up pictures of smiling faces. Avoid pictures of empty chairs and empty rooms.

Of course, make sure anyone you photograph is comfortable with their image being posted on social media. If they are a minor, always seek permission from a parent or legal guardian first.

Building Your Launch Team

There comes a moment in every church plant when things shift. Up until that point, it has been vision, planning, praying, and preparing. But then people begin to gather. A conversation turns into a connection. A connection turns into a Bible study. A Bible study turns into a small group. And suddenly, you are not just planting a church. You are pastoring people. Buildings don't carry the burden of the mission. People do. This is where the launch team becomes essential.

There are three primary models for planting an Apostolic church: the parachute model, the daughter work, and the launch model. Within each, there are also three approaches: the instant launch, building a team through Bible studies and small groups, and the launch team approach.[6]

The Parachute Model

The parachute model is when a family parachutes into a community to plant a church. Most Apostolic churches have been started this way. When my family relocated to Westchester County, New York, to start Westchester Apostolic Church, we used this model. Not because it was the best one, but because it was the only one available to us. The cost of living in the New York City metro area kept some willing families from coming.

Thankfully, Pastor Doug Davis released two wonderful families to come on alternating weekends our entire first year to help with music. I will always be eternally grateful to Robert and Deanna Cattani and Dan Crawford for making the sacrifice of driving an hour each way to support a brand-new church. After we received our pastor's blessing to go to New York, we began praying that God would give us a team, a town, and a time. We trusted Him to assemble the team, point us to the right town in Westchester County, and lead us to the right launch date. Once our boots hit the ground, God built that team through Bible studies and small groups.

Another approach, paired with the parachute model, is to begin services as soon as possible. I have seen this work in rural communities. In larger cities, the cost of securing a building usually leaves the church plant cash-strapped. Remember, if you focus on building the church, the resources for a building will follow. If you focus first on the building, you may never build the church.

If you focus on building the church, the resources for a building will follow. If you focus first on a building, you may never build a church.

The Daughter Work Model

A highly successful model is the daughter work, where a mother church embraces the challenge of planting a daughter congregation that will eventually become autonomous. The strength of this model is that the mother church naturally provides all three forms of support: prayer, finances, and a launch team. Service times are typically arranged so the launch team can still participate in the mother church's services and events during the early stages.

It is critical that the mother-daughter work plan be laid out in writing. Who pays the bills? Who decides who preaches? When will the daughter work become self-governing and self-supporting? Who from the mother church is helping? Are they on loan, and if so, for how long? The pastor of the mother church is the spiritual authority over the entire process. But putting everything in writing dramatically reduces the chances of misunderstanding down the road.

The Launch Model

The launch model uses community interest meetings to form a launch team. The launch team is not the core leadership of the new congregation. Their primary purpose is to recruit others to join the launch team, which will greatly increase the attendance of the new church. The launch team ceases to exist after the first service. Out of that team often come Bible studies, future disciples, and future leaders. Even in their pre-converted state, they help gather a group of non-Apostolics from the community who will experience the full Apostolic message for the first time.

No matter which model you use, build culture before you build crowds. What you tolerate early will multiply later. Model prayer, excellence, unity, faith, and integrity from day one. Whatever you establish in the early days will define the future of the church.

Always Be Ethical

As your team begins to grow, opportunities will arise. People from other churches may express interest in joining you. This is where your integrity will be tested.

If you would like Apostolics to join your launch team, talk to their pastor before you ever mention it to them. If their pastor is not comfortable with it, never, and I mean never, bring it up to them directly. Your integrity is more valuable than their help. If God has called you to plant a church, He will send you the help you need.

If their pastor releases them, find out whether they are on loan or being sent permanently. If they are on loan, for how long? Get the agreement in writing. The sending pastor always has the right to shorten or extend their tenure. The important thing is that you honor the original agreement unless the sending pastor adjusts it. It is better to build slowly with integrity than quickly with compromise. God does not need you to cut corners to accomplish His will.

One Small Step, One Giant Team

On July 20, 1969, Apollo 11 accomplished what humanity had never done before. A man walked on the moon. The world remembers Neil Armstrong. His name is etched into history. But Armstrong did not get there alone. Behind him stood over four hundred thousand people: engineers, mathematicians, technicians, flight controllers, seamstresses who stitched the suits, and programmers who wrote code before modern computers even existed.[7] At Mission Control in Houston, dozens of specialists watched every number, every signal, every fluctuation.

When Armstrong stepped onto the lunar surface, he said, "That's one small step for man, one giant leap for mankind." But the truth is, that step was not only his. It belonged to everyone who made it possible.

Church planting works the same way. One person may preach the first message. One family may carry the vision. But behind every thriving church is a team. Someone who prayed when no one was watching. Someone who gave when it stretched them. Someone who set up chairs before anyone arrived. Someone who believed when the results were small. When the church launches, when souls are baptized, when lives are filled with the Holy Ghost, the victory does not belong to one person. It belongs to the team.

Every great move of God may have a visible voice, but it always has an invisible army.

When you gather the right team, when prayer covers it, when sacrifice funds it, when people unite around it, you don't just launch a church. You launch something no single person could ever build alone. And that, my friend, is how the Kingdom of God advances.

Discussion & Application

Use these questions for personal reflection or group discussion.

1. Where in your current ministry are you trying to "stand tall" instead of staying connected? What specific roots, whether prayer, financial, or relational, need to grow outward this season?

2. The author argues that "your résumé will largely determine your resources." What does your ministry track record currently communicate to potential supporters, and what would you change if you could?

3. Of the three models presented, parachute, daughter work, and launch, which best fits your calling, your context, and the resources God has placed around you, and why?

4. The chapter draws a sharp line between asking God for personal wants and asking Him for what is needed to "get the job done." How does this distinction reshape the way you have been praying about provision?

5. Where have you been tempted to compromise integrity, perhaps by recruiting from another pastor's church without permission, because you felt pressure to grow quickly? What boundaries will you put in place going forward?

Chapter Eleven

First Things First

I n 1607, a group of settlers landed on the shores of what would become Jamestown, Virginia. They carried vision. They carried hope. They carried expectations of wealth. Many of them were gentlemen, educated, ambitious, and convinced that prosperity was waiting just beneath the soil. But they made a fatal mistake. Instead of securing food, building sustainable shelter, and learning the land, they spent their first days searching for gold. They chased what glittered instead of what sustained. And then winter came.

With winter came starvation, disease, and desperation. History now calls it "The Starving Time," and it nearly wiped out the colony. Some accounts even suggest cannibalism as settlers clawed to survive.[1] They did not fail because they lacked vision. They failed because they neglected the first things. That is not just American history. That is ministry reality.

Church planters rarely fail because they lack calling, passion, or gifting. They fail because they overlook the fundamentals. They chase the visible before securing the invisible. They focus on the launch before establishing their life. If you do not get the first things right, the weight of the calling will eventually expose what was never properly built.[2]

Church planters rarely fail because they lack calling. They fail because they chase what glitters instead of what sustains.

So before we talk about crowds, platforms, or launch dates, we have to talk about foundations. Every lasting move of God is built on something unseen. And the first thing God requires of every sent servant is not a sermon. It is an order.

Before the Pulpit, There Must Be a Place

A friend of mine once asked veteran missionary Benny DeMerchant what the first thing he did upon arriving in Brazil for the first time was. He smiled and said, "Well, the first thing I did was go to baggage claim and pick up my suitcases." I love that. That simple practicality is a necessity for every successful church planter. Before you preach, before you strategize, before you cast vision, somebody has got to pick up the suitcases. Before you can reach a city, you have to establish a home.

When you arrive in a new city, your first assignment is not preaching. It is positioning. Before there is a platform, there must be a place. You need a home that breathes peace. You need a space where your family can rest, recalibrate, and recover from the weight of transition. Moving is not merely logistical. It is psychological. It disorients routines, disrupts rhythms, and quietly drains emotional energy.

If your home is unsettled, your spirit will be unsettled. And if your spirit is unsettled, your leadership will reflect it. That is why securing a place to live is not a side task. It is a spiritual priority. Scripture reminds us that "God is not the author of confusion, but of peace" (1 Corinthians 14:33). Order is not the enemy of the Spirit. Order is the environment where the Spirit thrives. A chaotic home produces a distracted leader. A peaceful home produces a focused vessel. You cannot pour into a city if your own life is leaking.[3]

Unpacking Is Spiritual Work

It sounds simple. Maybe even mundane. Unpack the boxes. Yet many church planters delay this step. They live out of cardboard for weeks, sometimes months, because "ministry is busy." But every unopened box is a silent source of stress. Psychologists call it cognitive load, the mental weight carried by unfinished tasks.[4] When your environment is disorganized, your mind never fully rests. You are constantly processing what is incomplete.

That quiet tension shows up in your decisions and your relationships. Unpacking is not just about organizing your house. It is about settling your mind. It is telling your spirit, "We are here. We are planted. This is home." There is something deeply spiritual about hanging pictures, setting up your kitchen, and arranging your living space. You are not merely decorating. You are declaring permanence. You are saying, "God sent us here, and we are staying."

Let me speak to the planter's spouse for a moment. The one washing dishes in a kitchen full of boxes. The one comforting children who miss their old bedroom. Your work is not less than the work of the pulpit. It is the soil the pulpit grows in. When you create a home that feels like home, you are not serving in the background of the call. Heaven sees it, and heaven records it.

When the Moving Truck Pulls Away

There comes a quiet, terrifying moment in many church plants. The moving team has rolled away. The family members who flew in to help have caught their flights back home. The last friend waved goodbye from the driveway. And now, for the first time, it is just the planter and their family alone in a strange city. To this point, church planting has been about vision, fantasizing, and dreaming. It has been the fun part. But now the house is quiet, the boxes are half-opened, and a flood of questions begins to rise. "What have we gotten ourselves into?"

If that has been you, or if that will be you, I want you to hear me clearly. You are not the first one to feel it, and you will not be the last. Self-doubt is not a sign that you missed God. Often, it is a sign that the weight of what God called you to has finally become real. The vision that lived in your prayer closet now lives in your living room, and it feels heavier in person than it did in private. Do not panic. Do not pack up. Do not call the district superintendent and ask to come home.

In that moment, you must preach to yourself before you try to preach to a city. Remind yourself that you are called by God. Remind yourself that you are living your dream, even if your dream currently smells like cardboard and packing tape. Remind yourself that the One who sent you did not send you to fail. And whatever you do, do not start comparing yourself to other church planters, their talents, their gifts, their platforms, their results. Scripture warns us plainly that those who compare themselves among themselves are not wise.

Self-doubt is not a sign that you missed God. It is often a sign that the weight of the call has finally become real.

Be Who God Called You to Be

We carry some strong ideas about what a church planter is supposed to look like. We like to believe they must be an absolute people person. Outgoing. Magnetic. A room-filler. But one of the largest Apostolic churches planted in recent years was started by a man who is painfully introverted. We like to believe that a church planter must be an incredible soul-winner, a stage-level evangelist. But I can point you to a church planter who has started six successful churches and openly confesses, "I am not a harvester. I am a discipler. I told God years ago that if He would send me people, I could disciple them."

That is my story too. I am not a classic evangelist. I am a teacher, a trainer, a discipler, which are the giftings needed to be an effective pastor. Paul told Timothy to "do the work of an evangelist, make full proof of thy ministry" (2 Timothy 4:5), so if you are a pastor, you will have to do the work of an evangelist. But you do not have to be a superstar one. Home Bible studies are where every gifting gets to shine. If you are an evangelist, they play to your strength. If you are a discipler like me, then start discipling people before they ever get converted.[5]

The one thing you must be to plant a church is yourself. God will never hold you accountable for failing to be a better imitation of somebody else. Be who God created and called you to be. Either He will enable you to meet needs that are not naturally innate to you, or He will send others around you who will. Do your best to be secure enough to give those people the freedom to serve in their areas of giftedness within your new church community. God does not call the qualified. He qualifies the called.

Learn the City, Love the People

Now the boxes are unpacked. The pictures are hung. The self-doubt has been preached to and put in its place. It is time to step outside the front door. When Nehemiah arrived in Jerusalem, he did not call a meeting. He did not announce a plan. He did not gather a crowd. He went for a walk. At night. Quietly. Nehemiah 2 tells us he rode out under the cover of darkness to inspect the broken walls. He moved slowly, observing the burned gates, the crumbled stones, the places where the wall had collapsed.

Because he understood what every church planter must learn. You cannot build what you have not first understood. Nehemiah did not start with construction. He started with connection. With the land. With the condition. With the reality of the city he had been called to serve. And if you miss this step, you will build something, but it may not be what the city actually needs.[6]

Being a church planter is loving God, loving people, going into the world, and getting to know them. It is very practical. Do not overthink this. Step out of your front door and meet your neighbors. Learn their names. Begin praying for them every day, even before you know who they are. Pray for the house on the right, the house on the left, and the house across the street. If your children are in school, attend every school event you can. Meet as many parents as possible.

Go to the same grocery stores on purpose. Read the name tags of the workers who serve you, and call them by name. Go to the same restaurants. Go to the same coffee shops. There is no sweeter sound in all the world than the sound of a person's own name. You will become a source of emotional oxygen to them, and they will light up when they see you walk in the door. Before you gather a crowd, you must connect with individuals. Every handshake is a seed, and every conversation is soil.

Before you gather a crowd, you must connect with individuals. Every handshake is a seed, and every conversation is soil.

I am going to give you a strategy I used personally. I kept a note section in my phone for the restaurants we frequented. I wrote down every worker I met, their name, what country they were from, what college they attended, what sports they played, and what their major was. It helped me carry on real conversations every time I walked in. One time, there was an earthquake in Haiti, and several of the workers at our regular restaurant were from Haiti. I went by in the middle of the day, not to eat, but simply to check on my friends and ask about their families. That is ministry. That is Jesus with skin on.[7]

Meet the Felt Needs, Win the City

As you connect with a community, opportunities will open up to serve at the community level. While we were in New York, I had the privilege of serving on the Salvation Army Advisory Committee for the Tarrytown Corps. We soon discovered that street fairs were a major part of the rhythm of community life in Westchester County. Both Ossining, where we lived, and Tarrytown held large summer street fairs. Tarrytown held a street fair every third Friday of the month.

So we went. We set up a table and a tent, and we gave away free bottled water. Of course, we had our church material and promotional items there, but the real currency was presence. We were there. We were smiling. We were saying, in the quiet language of a bottle of cold water, that there was a church in their city that actually cared whether they were thirsty. Thetus Tenney once asked a question that has haunted me in the best way. If your church ceased to exist, would anybody in your community even care?

Think about that. Many established churches have been in their neighborhoods for decades, yet the community would still not notice if the lights went out. Because the community does not care about the worship services you conduct inside your building. They care about the difference you make in the streets outside of it. They care about the felt needs you are willing to meet. This is not some modern trick. This is totally Apostolic. Early church history tells us that first-century Christians would walk the forests where unwanted babies had been abandoned, pick them up, and adopt them as their own. The epistles breathe this spirit. Meet the needs of those around you.

Reaching Krakow One Conversation at a Time

Tony and Rhonda Adams went to Krakow, Poland, several years ago. They did not know the language. They did not know the people. They did not know the city. They simply went to establish an Apostolic church. One of the first doors that opened was an opportunity to work alongside a couple who owned a coffee shop. So they rolled up their sleeves and started serving, learning the city one cup at a time, learning the people one conversation at a time.

As time went on, they discovered that Poland, though largely Catholic, has a deep gospel choir culture. Rhonda Adams, a gifted musician and singer, stepped in and eventually joined the leadership of the Krakow Gospel Choir. Several choirs began using their church facilities for practice, which was absolutely brilliant. Because it has been said, and it is true, that if a person comes into your church for any reason, they will generally come back for another reason.

Then in 2022, the Russia-Ukraine war broke out. Refugees came pouring across the Polish border into Krakow by the thousands. And the Adams family was already positioned. They poured themselves into meeting needs, housing refugees, clothing them, feeding them, and helping them build a new life in a new country. Today, if you go to Krakow, you will find a strong, established Apostolic church, built in just a few years, on the foundation of felt needs faithfully met.

Feeding Families, Reaching a Nation

Toufic and April Azar went to Beirut, Lebanon. They had not been there long before she felt the burden to start a Christian school. You see, children in that country who were not Lebanese citizens were not allowed to attend public school. So the Azars opened the doors, and the school became a success. But the story did not stop there. As they taught those children, it became apparent that many of them were going home hungry. Food insecurity was real. And they discovered something powerful. For twenty-six dollars in U.S. currency, they could feed a family of four for an entire month with a single box of food.

So they started feeding families. And then more families. In time, the program grew to feed members of the Lebanese army and their families as well. That single act of compassion opened doors into the offices of high-level government officials in Lebanon, doors that money could never have bought. It is simply amazing what God has done through the Azars across the Middle East, in countries that looked closed to the gospel. But the doors opened because they walked in and met a felt need.

A Church That Lasts

So here is the order. First, you unpack the boxes and make a home. Second, you deal with the self-doubt that comes when everybody is gone, and it is just you and your family in a new city. Third, you find ways to connect with your city, to learn its name and let it learn yours. God did not send you to that place to survive. He sent you there to make an impact, to change that city positively with the gospel of Jesus Christ.[8]

There is a difference between a launch and a legacy. Anybody with a sound system and a social media account can gather a crowd for a Sunday. But it takes a shepherd who honors the first things to build something that still stands twenty years later. The enemy does not mind if you have a loud opening service. He trembles when you have a deep foundation. So do not be ashamed of the slow work. Do not apologize for the ordinary. Do not despise the day of small things.

Because crowds do not equal conversion. Attendance does not equal transformation. The early church gathered in the temple, yes, but the real discipleship happened from house to house (Acts 2:46). Large gatherings inspire, but small settings transform. If you want a church that lasts, you must build a church that teaches, one kitchen table at a time, one open Bible at a time, one soul at a time. Disciples are not mass-produced. They are personally developed.[9]

And when you finally stand on launch day, when the music is playing, and the first hands are lifted in worship, you will know the truth. What people are celebrating in public is the fruit of what you surrendered in private. The peaceful home. The unpacked boxes. The preached-to self-doubt. The walked neighborhoods. The bottle of cold water at a street fair. The phone note full of names. These were not small things. These were the first things. And because you honored them, God can now trust you with the next things. To God be the glory for a church built the right way, in the right order, for the right reasons.

Discussion & Application

Use these questions for personal reflection or group discussion.

1. Where in your current season are you tempted to chase the "gold" of visible success before securing the "food" of fundamentals, and what would it cost your family if you kept chasing?

2. If the moving truck pulled away today and self-doubt began to whisper, what specific truths would you need to preach to yourself, and who is in your life to help you hear them?

3. Be honest about your gift mix. Are you more of an evangelist or a discipler, and how have you been either hiding from or trying to imitate the opposite gifting instead of leaning into who God actually made you to be?

4. If your church ceased to exist tomorrow, would anyone in your community notice? Name one felt need in your city that you have the capacity to begin meeting in the next thirty days.

5. Looking at Tony and Rhonda Adams, Toufic and April Azar, and the street fairs of Westchester County, what is your version of a coffee shop, a gospel choir, a Christian school, or a bottle of cold water, and what is keeping you from starting?

Chapter Twelve

From Table to Transformation

In the heart of downtown Memphis, Tennessee, there is a beautiful thirty-acre park stretching along the eastern bank of the Mississippi River. Locals and tourists walk its paths, take in the panoramic view of the water, and admire the bridge arching across to Arkansas. The park bears a simple name. Tom Lee Park. For years, I was like most people who pass through. I knew the name on the sign, but I did not know the story behind it. It was not until God began dealing with me about pastoring in Memphis, and I started digging into the city's history, that I stumbled across a story that forever reframed the way I think about ministry.

On May 8, 1925, Tom Lee was piloting a small wooden boat called the Zev down the Mississippi River. He was a laborer, not a trained rescuer. He was not a professional. And perhaps most surprising of all, he could not swim. That day, a large vessel called the M.E. Norman was carrying engineers and their families. Then, without warning, the Norman capsized. In a matter of moments, dozens of men, women, and children were thrown into the muddy current, many of them trapped, injured, or unable to fight the river.[1]

Seventy-two lives hung in the balance. And Tom Lee saw it. He did not hesitate. He did not calculate the risk. He did not disqualify himself. He turned his boat around. Trip after trip, he pulled drowning passengers from the water, loading his little boat beyond what seemed reasonable, carrying them to the sandbar, and returning again. Thirty-two people lived that day because one man decided to reach. Later, with humility, he said, "I guess I didn't do any more than anyone else would have done."

Tom Lee could have disqualified himself a dozen ways. "I do not know how to swim. I do not have the training. I do not have the skills." Instead, with his actions, he said, "I may not be able to swim, but I can reach. I may not have every qualification I would like, but I can stretch my hand toward the drowning." And here is the truth every church planter must carry into every Bible study. If God has placed you in position, you are the most qualified person in the room to reach. Because you are there.

You Are the Light of the World

Jesus made a statement in Matthew 5:14 that ought to arrest every church planter. "Ye are the light of the world. A city that is set on an hill cannot be hid." This is the same Jesus who declared in John 8:12, "I am the light of the world." He said it during the Feast of Tabernacles, standing beneath sixteen massive oil lamps burning in the court of the women.[2] And now He turns to His followers and says, "You are the light." The mission did not end with Him. It continues through us.

Do not miss the weight of this. In Genesis 1:3, light was the first act of creation. "And God said, Let there be light: and there was light." Light announced the beginning of everything God was about to do. So when Jesus calls you the light of the world, He is saying something staggering. Where you walk, a new beginning becomes possible. Into workplaces. Into cubicles. Into neighborhoods. Into living rooms, around kitchen tables, and coffee shops, the potential for transformation walks in with you. You are carrying creation-level power into ordinary rooms.

Ten Principles for Effective Home Bible Studies

Every effective home Bible study I have ever seen was built on a framework. Not a script. Not a sales pitch. A framework. So let me give you ten principles that will shape every study you ever teach. These are not rigid rules. They are rhythms. Internalize them, and you will find that what once felt awkward begins to feel anointed, and what once felt mechanical begins to feel like ministry.

Principle One: Build Relationship Before You Build Revelation

Before people receive truth, they must trust you. Jesus modeled this on every page of the Gospels. He ate with Zacchaeus before He addressed his life. He sat at a well and asked a Samaritan woman for a drink before He revealed who He was. Relationship prepares the heart for revelation. Ineffective Bible studies open with, "Let us turn to lesson one." Effective ones open with, "How has your week been? How can I pray for you?" That is not small talk. That is soil preparation.[3]

Principle Two: Teach for Understanding, Not Completion

You will feel pressure to finish the chart, cover the material, and stay on pace. Resist it. Finishing a lesson is not the goal. Transformation is. You can complete every lesson and still miss the heart entirely. Jesus never rushed understanding. He paused. He asked questions. He made sure truth was received, not just delivered. After you read a verse, slow down. Let them process. It is not what you cover that matters. It is what they carry home.

Principle Three: Ask Questions

Stop trying to carry the conversation, and start guiding it. Jesus asked questions constantly, not because He needed information, but because questions engage the heart. Questions invite participation. They reveal understanding. They create ownership. Instead of saying, "Here is what this means," try asking, "What do you see happening here?" Because when they say it, they believe it more deeply. The strongest convictions are not imposed. They are discovered. And discovered truth has roots that pressured truth will never have.

The strongest convictions are never imposed. They are discovered, and discovered truth has roots that pressured truth will never have.

Principle Four: Create a Safe Environment for Honest Dialogue

People do not come to Bible studies as blank slates. They bring backgrounds. Traditions. Questions. Wounds. If they feel judged, they will shut down. And once they shut down, growth stops. Jesus was full of grace and truth, and you need both. Truth without grace feels harsh. Grace without truth feels empty. Instead of snapping, "That is wrong," try this. "That is a good question. Let us look at what the Scripture says." You can be right and still be ineffective if you are not relationally wise.

Principle Five: Let the Word Do the Work

You are not the source of transformation. The Word is. Hebrews 4:12 reminds us that "the word of God is quick, and powerful, and sharper than any twoedged sword." That means something supernatural is happening every time Scripture is read. Your role is to present truth clearly, ask questions wisely, and create space for the Spirit. God's role is to convict, to reveal, and to transform. A simple habit changes everything. Always read the Scripture aloud, and whenever possible, have them read it. Because when they read it, they will later say, "The Bible says," instead of, "You said."[4]

Principle Six: Recognize and Respond to Spiritual Hunger

Spiritual hunger rarely announces itself loudly. It shows up as curiosity. As a thoughtful question. As a willingness to linger after the study is over. As a tone that softens mid-sentence. Many church planters miss these moments because they are too focused on finishing the lesson. They stay on script when God is trying to move beyond it. Do not sacrifice a spiritual moment on the altar of your outline. When someone begins to open up, that is not the time to push ahead. That is the time to slow down and lean in.

Principle Seven: Handle Resistance Without Losing Relationship

At some point, every church planter will face resistance. "That is not what I was taught." "My church believes something different." "I am not sure about that." These moments can feel uncomfortable, but they are not negative. Resistance often signals engagement. People are thinking. Processing. Wrestling. If you respond defensively, you shut the door. If you respond harshly, you damage trust. But if you respond with grace and confidence, you keep the conversation open. Say, "I understand. That is a common perspective. Let us look at what the Scripture says." Always bring it back to the Word. You win people before you win perspectives.

Principle Eight: Lead People to a Decision

This is where many Bible studies quietly stall. They inform. They inspire. They even convict. But they never invite. And without invitation, conviction often fades into hesitation. You do not need to pressure people, but you cannot afford to avoid the moment. Jesus never manipulated, but He always called for response. "Follow me." "Go, and sin no more." Truth always carries an invitation. When you sense readiness, ask gently, "How do you feel about what we have studied? Would you like to take that step?" Unspoken conviction often becomes unresolved conviction.

Principle Nine: Understand That This Is How Churches Are Born

A home Bible study is never just a home Bible study. It is the seedbed of a church. Every person who repents, is baptized in Jesus' name, and is filled with the Holy Ghost is not just a convert. They are part of the foundation. What begins as one conversation, one study, and one family eventually becomes multiple studies, expanding relationships, and a growing circle of believers. Before there is ever a crowd, there is always a table. Revival is rarely built in a moment. It is built through consistency, week after week, study after study, conversation after conversation.[5]

Principle Ten: Follow Through Until Disciples Are Formed

The Bible study is not the finish line. It is the starting line of discipleship. Some of the most important moments will happen after the study is over. A text message. A follow-up conversation. Growth does not happen only in structured environments. It happens in reflection, ongoing conversation, and continued connection. The Bible study plants the seed. But follow-up waters it until disciples are formed.

Reach With Prayer

Sometimes reaching does not look like a scheduled Bible study at all. It looks like an errand. A routine stop. An ordinary weekday. I learned this the day I walked into the Bank of New York in Tarrytown to open a checking account for Westchester Apostolic Church. That was the whole plan. Open the account. Check the box. Get back to the office. I had no idea that God had already scheduled a divine appointment across a bank desk from me.

The young man helping me that day was named Andre Lundy. As we walked through the paperwork, the conversation drifted beyond deposits and signature cards. We connected. Something holy was happening in the middle of that bank lobby. Over the following weeks, that connection turned into a Bible study. That Bible study led to the waters of baptism in Jesus' name. And before long, I had the joy of praying him through to the infilling of the gift of the Holy Ghost. I thought I was running an errand. God was running a rescue mission.

But the story does not end there. A few months later, I had to tell Andre that I would not be available for our regular Bible study because I was attending a general conference in Richmond, Virginia. He froze. "Wait," he said, "my dad is going to be at a conference in Richmond, Virginia." Andre's parents had been divorced for years. He lived with his mother and grandmother, who were praying people, Pentecostal but not Apostolic. His father had lived in Virginia for a very long time. But his father had never stopped praying.

That is when I discovered the backstory. For years, his father had been crying out to God to send somebody to his son. Somebody who would lead him to the waters of baptism in the name of Jesus and pray him through to the infilling of the Holy Ghost. I was simply trying to open a checking account. I was unaware that I was walking straight into the answer of another man's prayer. You never know when a routine moment is actually a supernatural appointment. Somebody is praying. And you may be the answer walking through the door.

You never know when a routine moment is a supernatural appointment. Somebody is praying, and you may be the answer walking through the door.

God Uses Imperfect People

One of the most encouraging realities in soul-winning is this. God uses imperfect people. Let me tell you about a man named Joe Saragusa. Joe had been an alcoholic on Bourbon Street in New Orleans when God got a hold of his life and turned him around. He had been baptized in Jesus' name, filled with the Holy Ghost, and was actively involved in his church. But Joe was far from perfect. One day, he came home from work deeply troubled. His roommate asked what was wrong. Joe said, "You know that guy I have been witnessing to at work. We got into it today."

The roommate tried to calm him down. "Do not worry about it. You two will patch it up." Joe shook his head. "You do not understand. I knocked him out." Let that sit with you for a second. That is not exactly what we put in the soul-winning manual. But God did not disqualify Joe. Over time, Joe met and married a wonderful lady named Betty and moved to West Memphis, Arkansas. And then Joe began doing something quietly, week after week, that would echo through eternity. He started going into the Crittenden County Jail to teach the Word of God.

For the next thirty-five years, Joe walked into that jail with an open Bible. He baptized inmates in the name of Jesus. He prayed men through to the Holy Ghost. When Joe passed away a few years ago, the county sheriff posted something on Facebook that I will never forget. He said the jail had lost count. But their records indicated that over two thousand inmates had been baptized in the name of Jesus Christ through Joe's faithful ministry. Two thousand souls. From a man who once knocked out the person he was witnessing to.

God does not need you to be flawless. He needs you to be faithful with an open Bible in front of a hungry heart.

Here is the takeaway. God does not need you to be flawless. He needs you to be faithful. Joe Saragusa did not have a perfect testimony. But he had a willing spirit and an open Bible, and heaven has two thousand baptisms to prove it. J. T. Pugh once wrote that one soul is worth more than everything else on this planet put together. It is worth more than all the banks, all the stocks, all the real estate, and all the pleasures in this world combined. If that is true, and it is, then no bank lobby, no jail cell, and no kitchen table is beneath the dignity of a faithful home Bible study.

Don't Miss the Moment

There comes a moment in every effective home Bible study when teaching must give way to transformation. You can feel it before you hear it. The questions change. The posture shifts. The conversation moves from curiosity to conviction. Sometimes it arrives with tears. Sometimes it arrives with a long, quiet pause. And sometimes it arrives as a simple question that the student asks on their own. "So, when can I be baptized?" That moment is sacred, and every church planter must learn to recognize it when it comes. Because a Bible study is never just about information. It is about invitation. And the greatest tragedy is not a missed lesson. It is a missed moment.

Home Bible studies are not classrooms where we unload content and check boxes. They are sacred spaces where the Holy Ghost is actively working beneath the surface of every conversation. That means your job as the teacher is not only to deliver truth. It is to stay sensitive to what God is doing in your student's heart in real time. You have to watch their eyes. You have to notice the pause. You have to feel the weight in the room when Scripture lands on a place you did not even know was wounded. Because the Spirit of God is always a step ahead of your lesson plan.

Too many Bible studies stall, not because the teacher refused to baptize, but because the teacher was so focused on finishing the outline that they missed what God was already finishing in the student. So when you sense the Spirit moving, stop teaching and start asking. "How do you feel about what we have studied tonight? Is there anything holding you back from taking that step? Would you like to be baptized in Jesus' name?" These are not pressure questions. They are clarifying questions. They simply give voice to what the Holy Ghost is already whispering inside them. The goal of a Bible study was never just to transfer information from your notes to their notebook. The goal is transformation.

When No One Reaches

Sixty years before Tom Lee turned his little boat around, another tragedy unfolded on that same Mississippi River, just seven miles north of Memphis. The Sultana. A steamboat designed to carry 376 passengers was overloaded with more than 2,400 souls, many of them Civil War soldiers finally heading home after years of captivity. In the early morning hours of April 27, 1865, three of her four boilers exploded. Fire erupted. Panic spread. Within minutes, the ship was destroyed. An estimated 1,700 people perished. It remains the deadliest maritime disaster in United States history.[6]

And here is the haunting difference. There was no one there to reach. The explosion happened near two in the morning. It was not until three in the morning, a full hour later, that another vessel finally arrived on the scene. By then, for most of those men, it was too late. The Norman had Tom Lee. The Sultana had no one. And listen, that is the grief that ought to grip every church planter when we think about our cities. All around you, right now, in the house next door, in the cubicle beside you, in the car at the next stoplight, are men, women, boys, and girls drowning.

They are drowning in confusion. Drowning in sin. Drowning in hopelessness. They may never say it out loud, but their lives are crying out a question. "Will somebody reach for me?" And the question God asks you in return is not, "Are you perfect?" It is not, "Are you fully prepared?" It is not, "Do you have every answer memorized?" The question is simply this. "Are you willing?" Because just like Tom Lee, you may not feel like you can swim. But you can reach. And when you reach, and when you teach, and when people respond, something sacred begins to form.

Not just a Bible study. A people. A body. A church. What has been happening quietly in homes will eventually step into the open. The first service. The first time voices lift together in worship. The first time the vision becomes visible. But never forget how you got there. That moment was not built on a platform. It was built at a kitchen table. It was built in a coffee shop. Before there is ever a service, there is a soul. So reach with care. Reach with prayer. Reach with the Word. And shine on, church planter. Shine on, until Jesus comes.

Discussion & Application

Use these questions for personal reflection or group discussion.

1. Tom Lee could not swim, but he could reach. What disqualifications have you been using to excuse yourself from leading home Bible studies, and how does his example confront those excuses?

2. Look honestly at the ten principles in this chapter. Which one do you practice best, and which one do you most often neglect? What would it cost the people you are teaching if you never grew in that weak area?

3. Meeting Andre Lundy was the answer to his father's prayers, and I did not know it. Who in your current sphere may already be the subject of someone else's intercession, and how does that reality change your urgency this week?

4. Joe Saragusa saw more than two thousand baptisms come out of a county jail despite an imperfect testimony. What past failures have you allowed to silence your witness, and what would it look like to surrender those failures to God?

5. The strength of your first service will be determined by what is built in living rooms. Practically, how many active home Bible studies are you currently leading or overseeing, and what is one concrete step you will take in the next seven days to add one more?

Chapter Thirteen

The First Service

In September of 1857, a businessman named Jeremiah Lanphier put out a simple invitation in New York City. A weekly prayer meeting. Noon. All are welcome. The first day, nobody came at noon. He waited. Thirty minutes passed. Finally, one man walked in. Then another. Then a third. By the end of the hour, there were six. Six people in a room. No worship team. No stage. No momentum. Just six people praying.[1]

It would have been easy to call it a failure. Easy to wait for a better moment, a bigger crowd, a stronger start. But they came back the next week. And the next. Within months, that small gathering became a daily prayer movement. Thousands gathered across New York City. Businesses paused at noon so people could pray. Ships arriving in the harbor reported that passengers were already under conviction before stepping ashore. Historians would later call it the Layman's Prayer Revival, one of the most significant spiritual awakenings in American history. But it did not start with thousands. It started with six.

Great moves of God rarely begin with crowds. They begin with commitment, and heaven has never been intimidated by a small room.

Lanphier did not have a platform. He had a decision. He had decided ahead of time that the size of the crowd would not determine the faithfulness of the servant. You do not need a crowd to have a movement. You need a committed servant in a prepared room, and you need to keep showing up until God shows up. Every church planter eventually faces their own six-people-in-a-room moment. Not in theory. In reality. And what you decide in that moment will shape everything that comes after it.

More Than a Service, It Is a Statement

Your first service is not just an event on a calendar. It is a spiritual line in the sand. It declares to your city, "There is now a witness here." It declares to hell, "You no longer have uncontested ground." And it declares to you, the church planter, "The calling is no longer a conversation. It is a reality." Your first service may look small. But heaven never measures a moment by attendance. Heaven measures moments by alignment.

Scripture reveals a consistent pattern. God meets prepared places. In Acts 2, the disciples were "all with one accord in one place" when the Spirit fell. In 1 Kings 18, Elijah did not just pray for fire. He repaired the altar first. In Genesis 12, Abraham did not just receive promises. He built altars wherever he went. Before there is ever a move of God, there is always preparation. And that is what your first service represents. It is the culmination of the prayers you have prayed, the steps you have taken, the sacrifices you have made, and the obedience you have walked out. God honors prepared altars.[2]

Here is a leadership principle you cannot afford to miss. Preparation creates capacity. Passion without preparation produces frustration, but preparation creates capacity for what God wants to do. If you prepare intentionally, people will feel it, and your team will be strengthened by it. If you neglect preparation, confusion will replace clarity, and opportunity will be missed. Faith is not a substitute for preparation. Faith fuels preparation.

The Invisible Work Before the Visible Moment

Before your first service ever begins, there is a layer of work that no one sees, but everyone will feel the impact of. This is where many church planters either build strength or create unnecessary struggle. You are not just launching a service. You are establishing a church. Spiritual passion must be paired with practical wisdom. It may feel strange to talk about incorporation and insurance in the same breath as worship and revival. But both matter. What you are building is not just a moment. It is a ministry. And ministries require both spiritual fire and structural integrity.

You can have a powerful service without structure. But you cannot sustain a powerful church without it.[3]

One: Establish Legal Formation

At a basic level, your church should be established as a legal entity. This typically includes incorporating as a nonprofit organization and establishing foundational governance documents such as bylaws. This is not about red tape. This is about responsibility. It protects you. It protects your family. It protects the church. Do not put this off until it feels convenient. The longer you wait, the messier it gets. Get it done before your first offering is ever received.

Two: Obtain a Federal Identification Number

An Employer Identification Number, or EIN, is necessary for opening a bank account and handling financial operations. It is simple to obtain, but absolutely essential. You cannot run a church's finances through your personal checking account, and you should not want to. Get the EIN. Open a separate, dedicated church bank account. Keep the lines clean from day one. Your future self will thank you, and your auditors, if the day ever comes that you have auditors, will bless your name.

Three: Build Financial Integrity Systems

Before you receive a single dollar in offerings, you need a dedicated church bank account, a reliable system for tracking contributions, and clear offering-handling procedures. Never, ever let one person handle the offering alone. Two sets of eyes on every dollar is not distrust. It is wisdom. Integrity is not something you fix later. It is something you build from the very beginning. Financial scandals in the church rarely begin with theft. They begin with sloppy systems that enable theft. Tighten the systems now, while they are still small, and you will never have to untangle them later.

Four: Secure Insurance and Manage Risk

At a minimum, you need to explore general liability insurance and coverage for your meeting location. You are not expecting problems. You are preparing to withstand them. A child falls on a slippery floor. A guest slips in the parking lot. A storm damages your rented space. These things happen, and they happen to ministries that love God as much as you do. Insurance is not a lack of faith. It is an act of stewardship. Protect the sheep God has entrusted to you by protecting the structure that shelters them.

Five: Seek Professional Guidance

Do not try to navigate legal and financial matters alone. Work with a qualified public accountant. Work with a qualified legal professional. Laws change. Regulations shift. Every state is different. This book is not your legal manual. Your denominational headquarters and your district office often have resources and referrals for planters in exactly your situation. Use them. Ask for help. A humble phone call today can save you a decade of headaches tomorrow.

Spiritual passion must be paired with practical wisdom. A powerful service needs no structure, but a powerful church cannot survive without it.

Hot Church in a Cold Room

Now let me tell you a story about what happens when preparation meets presence. The high temperatures in the New York City metro area during the first two weeks of January 2012 ranged from 30 to 60 degrees. Downright toasty for January in New York. But on Sunday, January 15, we were thrown straight into the deep freeze. At church time, the thermostat outside read in the teens. To make matters worse, it was a three-day holiday weekend. And during our regularly scheduled service time, the New York Giants were playing the Green Bay Packers for the right to advance to the NFC Championship Game. The church planter's perfect storm was brewing.

Then came the straw that should have broken the camel's back. The heat in the building we used for services was not working. When we walked in to set up, the sanctuary was fifty-two degrees. When we left five hours later, it was a balmy fifty-five. Frigid temps. Strike one. Three-day weekend. Strike two. Giants in the playoffs. Strike three. No heat. Strike four. Wait, we were already out. But something holy happened that day. The people who came, came to worship. It was not the most demonstrative service we ever had, but it was heartfelt and God-glorifying. We refused to concede the moment. When it was over, people kept saying the same thing. "Pastor, it was cold in here, but we had hot church!"

Here is what I learned that day. The enemy will always try to sabotage your services with circumstances. A storm will blow in. The sound system will cut out. The furnace will quit on the coldest Sunday of the year. These are not signs God is against you. They are invitations to find out whether you will worship Him anyway. John Grant once told me that a key to building a great church is to never have a wasted church service. Easier said than done, right? Not really, when you understand what it actually takes.

Every year holds fifty-two Sundays. Some services will be home runs. Others will be triples, doubles, or singles. Sometimes you will get on base with a bunt or an error. But never, never, never give up on a service. View each year of services as one long baseball game. If you get on base every Sunday, the church wins big in the end. You cannot hit grand slams without base runners. Your job on any given Sunday is not to manufacture a miracle. Your job is to get on base. Preach the Word. Worship in spirit and in truth. Love the people. Trust God for the win.

Three Marks of a Service That Is Never Wasted

Every effective service I have ever led was built on a framework. Hit these three marks every single Sunday, and I promise you, you will never walk away saying the service was wasted. Miss them, and it will not matter how many people showed up or how smooth the transitions felt. The scoreboard of heaven is not measured in production quality. It is measured in presence, love, and the Word.

One: Every Service Should Experience the Love of God

This happens naturally when we enter genuine worship and praise. Heartfelt worship is not built on good music, excellent sound, or outstanding video production. There will be Sundays when the music is off, the sound fights you, and the video is on the blink. Yet if hearts are right, God's love and presence will fill that room anyway. People do not come to be impressed. They come to be touched. And God is always ready to touch a hungry heart long before the sound tech finds the right cable.

Two: Every Service Should Experience the Love of the Church

Jesus said, "By this shall all men know that ye are my disciples, if ye have love one to another" (John 13:35). Expressing genuine love for one another should be a vital part of every service. Love cannot remain a slogan on a welcome card. It must become a lived experience in the room. Guests should feel it before the first song ends, and regulars should carry it home after the final amen.[4]

Three: Every Service Should Experience a Clearly Communicated Word From God

There will be times when you feel you communicated the gospel better than at other times. That is part of the journey. But the real question is not whether you preached the most eloquent sermon of your life. The real question is this. Did you clearly communicate the message God gave you to deliver? If so, be confident in your efforts. Romans 10:17 reminds us that "faith cometh by hearing, and hearing by the word of God." Clarity matters more than cleverness. A clear message is always more powerful than a clever one. Any service that genuinely accomplishes these three marks is a success.

Every Role Shapes the Outcome

You are not doing ministry alone. You are building a ministry through people. Every role in that first service matters. Not because you need perfection, but because people experience what is actually happening, not what you intended to happen. You may intend to be welcoming, but if no one greets guests, it will not be felt. You may intend to create a powerful worship atmosphere, but if your team is disengaged, it will not be experienced. You may intend to preach clearly, but if distractions dominate, the message may not land. Execution shapes experience. Let me walk you through the key roles that must be filled before your first Sunday.

Ushers and Greeters: The Ministry of the First Impression

Before anyone hears a sermon, they feel something. The entrance. The first handshake. These moments matter more than most church planters realize. A confident greeting, a genuine smile, and clear direction are not small tasks. They are ministry. People often decide whether they are coming back before the first song ever begins. Recruit your warmest people for this role and train them to watch for the nervous first-time guest. This is not just a volunteer spot. This is a ministry assignment.

Worship Team: Creating Space for God to Move

Worship is not filler. It is formation. It shapes the spiritual environment of the entire room. In 2 Chronicles 5, when the musicians and singers were "as one," the glory of the Lord filled the house so powerfully that the priests could not stand to minister. Unity invites glory. Your worship team does not need to be large or highly polished. But they must be prayerful, engaged, and unified. Authenticity will always outweigh performance. You are not trying to impress people. You are trying to invite God. A small team that is in one accord will always be more powerful than a large team full of hidden tensions.[5]

Preacher: The Anchor of the Service

At the center of every effective service is the Word of God. Your first message sets a tone, not just stylistically but spiritually. Preach with clarity so they understand it. Preach with conviction so they feel it. Preach with direction so they know what to do next. This is not the time for complexity. It is the time for connection. Do not try to download everything you know about the Book of Revelation into one Sunday morning. Preach one clear truth from one clear text with one clear invitation, and trust God to do the rest.

Altar Workers: The Purpose of the Moment

Every service should lead somewhere. In Acts 2, when conviction hit, the people asked, "Men and brethren, what shall we do?" Peter did not hesitate. He gave them a response. Your first service must include a clear opportunity for people to respond, to pray, to repent, to step forward. Do not rush this moment. This is why the church exists. Train a handful of Spirit-filled altar workers ahead of time. Teach them how to pray someone into repentance and through to the Holy Ghost. This role is too important to leave to chance.

Children's Ministry: Reaching the Whole Family

Healthy churches think generationally from day one. If a family visits your church, they are not just evaluating the service. They are evaluating whether this is a place for their children. Your children's ministry should communicate safety, care, and intentionality. It does not have to be elaborate, but it must be organized, prepared, and thoughtful. When you reach a child, you often open the door to reach a whole family. Treat children's ministry as a mission field, because that is exactly what it is.

Audio/Visual and Production: Eliminating Distractions

Production should never be the focus, but it always affects the experience. If people cannot hear clearly, they disengage. If visuals are distracting, attention drifts. The goal is not to impress. The goal is to remove barriers. The best production is the kind people never notice. Recruit someone reliable and teachable for this role, even if they are not a professional.

Offering Handlers: Establishing a Culture of Generosity

Your first offering sets a precedent. This is not about pressure. It is about discipleship. From the beginning, teach your people why we give, what giving accomplishes, and how it honors God. Make sure your systems are ready from day one: secure handling, accountability in counting, and at least two people present at all times. Financial integrity builds trust, and trust strengthens ministry.

I Refuse to Pastor a Small Church

My wife and I started Westchester Apostolic Church in November of 2003 with a core group of a whopping seven people. Yet I have never been the pastor of a small church. That original core group could have fit comfortably into a standard-size minivan, yet I have never led a small congregation. In our first year, we conducted weekend services in seven different locations, but I have never been involved in planting a tiny, transient church. In those early days, it was hard to look people in the eyes while preaching a challenging sermon. It was always too easy to guess who I was talking about.

Zechariah declares, "For who hath despised the day of small things?" To my knowledge, we never did. Our mantra was simple. "One day, we are going to look back and call these the good old days. So let us choose to call them the best of days right now." Enjoy the close fellowship. Enjoy the community. Enjoy the intimacy. Those things will be difficult to maintain as your congregation grows. We have often said it this way. We are not a small church. We are a great church in its infancy. There is a massive difference between a small church and an infant church. An infant church is packed with promise and a future. A small church is defined by small thinking.[6]

There is a massive difference between a small church and an infant church. An infant church is packed with promise. A small church is defined by small thinking.

If you think like a small church, you will do church like a small church. You will act like one. You will pray like one. You will believe like one. More than likely, you will remain one. You will become grasshoppers in your own eyes. But if you think like a great church, you will be a great church. You will have great worship, great prayer, great altar services, great evangelism, and great fellowship. Your beginnings may seem small to outsiders, but your vision will be enormous.

The way you talk about your church in private is the way your church will grow in public. Stop apologizing for your size. Start speaking like the pastor of a great church in its infancy. Speak faith. Speak vision. Speak future. The words you use about your church today will become the walls or the windows of your church tomorrow.

From a Handful to a Harvest

In 1906, a small group of believers gathered in a humble building on Azusa Street in Los Angeles. It was not impressive. The structure had once been a stable. The floors were rough. The seating was makeshift. There was no platform to speak of and no polished presentation. At the center of it all was a one-eyed preacher named William J. Seymour, who often prayed with his head inside a wooden crate. No spotlight. No branding. No strategy sessions. Just prayer. Just hunger. Just a deep desire for God to move.

The first gatherings were small. Unpredictable. Unstructured. But something began to happen. The Spirit of God fell. People repented. People worshiped. People experienced the power of God in undeniable ways. Word spread, not through marketing, but through testimony. People came from across the city, then across the nation, then across the world. What started in that small, unimpressive space became known as the Azusa Street Revival, a movement that ignited Pentecostal fire across the globe. Millions would ultimately be impacted. But it started in a room most people would have walked right past.

Your first service may feel a lot like Azusa Street. Unpolished. Imperfect. Simple. But heaven has never been intimidated by humble beginnings. God does not require impressive environments. He responds to hungry hearts. You will feel pressure in your first service. Pressure to perform. Pressure to impress. Release that. You are not there to prove anything. You are there to be faithful. Carry this mindset: you are not leading a small church. You are leading a great church in its infancy. And God has never been embarrassed by an infant.

So prepare the room. Handle the paperwork. File the articles of incorporation. Secure the insurance. Recruit the team. Turn on whatever heat you have. Greet every guest like they are family. Worship with all your heart, whether there are six or sixty or six hundred in the chairs. Preach the Word clearly. Give the altar the time it deserves. And when the final amen is spoken, do not measure the service by the temperature of the room. Measure it by the love of God, the love of the church, and the Word of the Lord. A service that carries those three things is never wasted, and a church planter who stays faithful to those three things will never be ashamed.

Discussion & Application

Use these questions for personal reflection or group discussion.

1. Look honestly at the invisible work of your church plant. Which legal and financial foundations (incorporation, EIN, bank accounts, insurance, professional counsel) are still missing, and what is your timeline for putting each one in place before your first service?

2. Walk through the seven key ministry roles in this chapter: greeters, worship, preaching, altar workers, children's ministry, production, and offering handlers. Which role is your strongest right now, and which one exposes the greatest vulnerability in your first service?

3. Evaluate your last four services against the three marks of a service that is never wasted. Which of the three shows up most reliably, and which one is quietly being neglected while you chase production or attendance?

4. The difference between a "small church" and an "infant church" is mindset. Where in your prayers, budgets, planning, and language are you revealing grasshopper thinking, and what specifically will you change this week to start leading a great church in its infancy?

5. Jeremiah Lanphier showed up for six people, and William J. Seymour prayed with his head in a crate. If God asked you to be equally faithful in a room just as small, what fears would you have to crucify before you could say yes with your whole heart?

Chapter Fourteen

Developing a Culture of Discipleship

I n 1979, a group of engineers at a Japanese manufacturing plant was tasked with improving production quality. They did not begin with machinery. They did not start with budgets. They did not even begin with strategy. They started with culture. Every morning, before a single part was produced, employees gathered in small circles. No rank. No hierarchy. No fear. If something was broken, it was addressed immediately. If someone had an idea, it was honored. If a mistake was made, it was owned. Over time, something remarkable happened. Defect rates plummeted. Productivity soared. But more importantly, the people changed.

Years later, when outside consultants tried to replicate those results in other plants, they failed. Because they copied the systems, but they did not build the culture. The systems were visible. The culture was invisible. And the invisible always wins. That is the challenge of discipleship. You can build systems for follow-up. You can create classes. You can design pathways. But if you do not build a culture of discipleship, those systems will eventually collapse under the weight of inconsistency. What you celebrate becomes culture, and what becomes culture determines what grows. Samuel Chand said it best. "Culture trumps vision."[1]

You don't get what you preach. You get what you permit and what you model, because culture always trumps vision.

Culture is the most powerful and often the most overlooked force in any church. It is unseen, unspoken, and unexamined. Yet it determines how people respond to leadership, how guests are treated, how disciples are formed, and how leaders are developed. You can preach vision all day long, but if your culture contradicts your message, culture will win every time. So the question is not, "Do we believe in discipleship?" The real question is, "Is discipleship the culture of our church?" Because if discipleship is not intentionally built into the DNA of your church, it will never naturally occur at the level required to sustain revival.

A Culture of Immediate Connection

Every church planter must answer one question with painful honesty. What happens to someone after their first visit? If you do not have a clear answer, you do not have a discipleship strategy. You have a hope. One of the most powerful discipleship tools you have is not your pulpit. It is your follow-up. Years ago, I sent a simple handwritten card to a first-time guest named Joseph. It was not complicated. It was personal. "Joseph, it was great to have you with us Sunday. I would love to get together with you for coffee. Please know that you are in my thoughts and prayers."

Twenty years later, Joseph sent me a picture of that card. Twenty years. Let that sink in. We live in a world of instant messages, forgotten texts, and disposable communication, yet something handwritten, intentional, and sincere still carries weight across decades. Because discipleship begins with value. And people do not stay where they are not valued. If you lose someone in the first three days, you will rarely recover them. That means your church must build a culture of immediate connection, not eventually, but immediately, starting with the very first Sunday somebody walks through your door.

One Approach to the First Seventy-Two Hours

Let me share one framework that has worked well, but understand up front that there are many effective ways to follow up on guests. What matters most is that you actually do it, consistently, with warmth and intentionality. Take these ideas as a starting point and shape them to fit your context, your culture, and your team.

One rhythm that has served many church planters looks something like this. A same-day touch is a simple personal text within hours of the service, thanking them for attending. A next-day reinforcement is a follow-up message that references something from the service and offers a clear next step. A personal invitation within three to five days extends something relational, like coffee, a meal, or a home connection. And a handwritten note, rare as it is in our day, carries weight precisely because almost nobody does it anymore.

A framework like this is only a skeleton. Some churches follow up beautifully with a completely different rhythm. Some use digital tools. Some rely heavily on small group leaders. Some build everything around a hospitality team. The method is not sacred. The heart behind it is.

If follow-up is only a system, it will eventually break down. If it becomes part of the culture, it will multiply on its own. The goal is never for the pastor to carry this alone. The goal is for the entire church to feel responsible for every guest who walks through the door.

Whatever shape your approach takes, a few principles tend to hold true across the board. Reach out quickly, ideally within the first day, while the visit is still fresh. On a second visit, move the relationship forward with something personal like coffee or a meal. And do not wait too long before inviting them into a Bible study or small group where real discipleship can begin. Beyond that, trust the Holy Ghost, know your city, and build a rhythm that fits who God has called you to be.

The One Thing We Are Called to Do

At its core, discipleship is not optional. It is the mission. Jesus said in Luke 19:10, "For the Son of man is come to seek and to save that which was lost." That was His mission. But in Matthew 28:19, He passed the baton to us. "Go ye therefore, and teach all nations, baptizing them in the name of the Father, and of the Son, and of the Holy Ghost." Notice the shift. Jesus came to seek and save. We are called to make disciples. The job description of Jesus was evangelism. The church's job description is discipleship. Of course, you cannot have discipleship without conversion. And you do not truly have conversion unless it leads to discipleship.

Most people define a disciple as a student. That is not wrong, but it is incomplete. A student learns information. A disciple becomes an imitation. Paul said, "And you should imitate me, just as I imitate Christ" (1 Corinthians 11:1, NLT). That changes everything. A disciple is not just someone who knows truth, understands doctrine, and can answer questions. A disciple is someone who lives differently, thinks differently, and follows consistently. Discipleship begins with education, but it must lead to imitation.[2]

Discipleship begins with education, but it must lead to imitation.

We live in a generation that prefers convenience over commitment, experience over transformation, and programs over process. The result? We have churches full of attendees but not enough disciples. We have people who attend regularly, enjoy community, and appreciate preaching, but have never fully surrendered, fully followed, or fully reproduced. Dietrich Bonhoeffer warned us, "We must not make cheap what cost God everything."[3] True discipleship will cost something. Time. Energy. Relationship. Sacrifice. But anything that does not cost much will not produce much.

Who Is Your One?

Here is a principle you must never forget. You do not build a discipleship culture through programs. You build it through people. More specifically, you build it through your personal example. If you are not making disciples personally, your church will not make disciples corporately. You cannot delegate what you do not demonstrate. Before you ask, "Who is our outreach director?" or "Who is leading follow-up?", you must first ask, "Who is my one?" Who are you personally discipling right now? Because discipleship is not a department. It is a lifestyle. And lifestyles are caught more than they are taught.

Let me make this practical. Every leader in your church should be able to answer one question. "Who is your one?" One person you are praying for. One person you are investing in. One person you are walking with. Stan Gleason puts it this way: If one person wins one soul every day for thirty years, that is over ten thousand people. Impressive. But if one person disciples one person per year, and that process multiplies, you reach over a billion people within thirty years.[4] Because disciples reproduce. Converts attend. Disciples multiply. There is no revival lottery. There are no shortcuts.

We are not called to build big churches. We are called to build strong disciples, and big churches sometimes are the byproduct.

The Pathway: From Doctrine to Distinction

Vision without a pathway creates frustration. People do not need more inspiration. They need direction. So let me give you a clear, reproducible blueprint for turning a first-time guest into a fully formed Apostolic disciple. I frame it through two lenses that work together. The three D's: doctrine, distinction, and demonstration. What they believe, how they live, and who they become. And the three P's: principle, practice, and power. What Scripture teaches, what they apply daily, and what the Spirit produces in them. These are not separate tracks. They are intertwined. When they are working together, you produce a disciple who is grounded, growing, and reproducing.

Stage One: Doctrine and Principle

Every disciple's journey begins with truth. Jesus said in John 8:32, "Ye shall know the truth, and the truth shall make you free." Freedom does not begin with emotion. It begins with revelation. This is why the early church was built on teaching. Acts 2:42 says they "continued stedfastly in the apostles' doctrine." Before there was structure, there was doctrine. Before there was expansion, there was teaching. This is where the home Bible study becomes essential. Not optional. Not supplemental. Essential. Because discipleship is built best in circles, not rows.

At this stage, your focus is clear. You teach core Apostolic doctrine: the oneness of God, the name of Jesus, repentance, water baptism in Jesus' name, and the infilling of the Holy Ghost. You also teach foundational biblical truths: the authority of Scripture, identity in Christ, the nature of sin and redemption, the necessity of obedience, and the necessity of holiness. Do not just teach what is right. Teach why it matters. Because conviction is built on understanding. Disciples are not developed accidentally. They are developed intentionally. If you do not create environments where truth is taught personally and consistently, you will produce shallow believers, and shallow believers cannot sustain revival.

Stage Two: Distinction and Practice

Once truth is established, the next step is transformation. James 1:22 says, "Be ye doers of the word, and not hearers only, deceiving your own selves." This is where many discipleship efforts break down. People hear truth. They agree with truth. They even love truth. But they never apply truth. And truth that is not applied will eventually be abandoned. This is where discipleship becomes deeply personal. People do not just need instruction. They need an example. Paul said, "Be ye followers of me." That means discipleship is not just, "Here is what the Bible says." It is also, "Here is how I live it."[5]

Let me give you three practical areas where distinction must occur. First, daily devotion. Teach them how to pray, read the Word, and hear God's voice. But more importantly, show them. Pray with them. Read Scripture with them. Let them see your consistency. Disciples do not do what you say. They do what you model. Second, faithfulness to the house of God. Hebrews 10:25 warns against "forsaking the assembling of ourselves together." Faithfulness is not a rule. It is lifeblood. If you can miss church without being missed, something is missing. Third, lifestyle transformation, which includes holiness, integrity, speech, and conduct. But approach this carefully. Do not start with rules. Start with relationship. Transformation flows from relationship, not the other way around.

The Bummer Lamb

Let me give you a powerful illustration. In shepherding, there is something called a "bummer lamb." It is a lamb rejected by its mother. When that happens, the shepherd takes the lamb into his own home. He feeds it by hand. He wraps it in blankets. He holds it close so it can hear his heartbeat. Over time, the lamb grows strong. Eventually, it is returned to the field. But something is different. That lamb knows the shepherd's voice more intimately than any other sheep in the flock. When the shepherd calls, guess who runs first? The one who was personally cared for.

That is discipleship. People are often rejected, wounded, and distrustful. They do not need a program. They need a shepherd. And when you invest personally in someone, they grow stronger, connect more deeply, and follow more faithfully. Discipleship is not mass production. It is personal investment. It is hand-feeding the rejected until they can feed themselves. It is wrapping the wounded until they can stand in the field. It is holding the distrusting close enough to your heartbeat that they finally learn the sound of the Shepherd's voice.

Stage Three: Demonstration and Power

At this stage, something shifts. The disciple is no longer just learning truth or applying truth. They are becoming something different. Jesus said in Matthew 5:16, "Let your light so shine before men, that they may see your good works, and glorify your Father which is in heaven." Notice, it does not say turn your light on occasionally. It says let it shine. Because transformation has become identity. This is where the power component comes in. True Apostolic discipleship is not just behavior-driven. It is Spirit-empowered. Without the Spirit, doctrine becomes dry, practice becomes mechanical, and distinction becomes performance. But with the Spirit, doctrine comes alive, practice becomes natural, and distinction becomes authentic.

How do you know someone is reaching this stage? You begin to see a hunger for God, a sensitivity to the Spirit, a burden for lost people, a desire to serve, and a willingness to sacrifice. And most importantly, they begin to reproduce. Because mature disciples do not just grow. They multiply. Healthy things grow, but only mature things reproduce. Your job as a church planter is not just to grow people. Your job is to mature them to the point that they can reproduce themselves in someone else. That is the evidence that discipleship has fully taken root.

Deliver, Develop, Deploy

Everything we have talked about comes together in three simple words that describe the engine of Apostolic discipleship. Deliver. Develop. Deploy. First, God delivers people. From sin. From bondage. Into salvation. Second, you develop them. Through teaching. Through relationship. Through accountability. Third, you deploy them. Into ministry. Into leadership. Into disciple-making. If your process stops at development, you create consumers. If it continues all the way to deployment, you create contributors. And contributors build churches. Consumers drain them. You must decide which one your culture is actually producing, because your process will always reveal your priorities.

The goal of discipleship is not completion. It is reproduction. You are not raising followers of yourself. You are raising followers of Jesus who can lead others to Jesus. If your disciples are not discipling someone else within a reasonable period, your process is incomplete. That is where many church planters plateau. They win people. They teach people. They even develop people. But they fail to release people. And the same fear that keeps a parent from letting a child leave home is the same fear that keeps a pastor from releasing a disciple into ministry. Release is not loss. Release is multiplication.

From Disciple to Multiplier

If discipleship is the heartbeat of a church, then leadership development is its multiplication system. You can gather a crowd. You can grow a church. But you cannot sustain revival without leaders. Many growing church eventually hits a ceiling, not because of a lack of people, but because of a lack of leadership. So the question becomes, how do we move someone from disciple to leader? Two commissions shape everything we do. The first commission in Genesis 1:28. "Be fruitful, and multiply." The great commission in

Matthew 28:19. "Go ye therefore, and teach all nations." Put them together, and you get the full picture. We are called to multiply disciples who multiply disciples.

I summarize the whole journey in three words. Reach. Teach. Release. Reach is evangelism. Teach is discipleship. Release is leadership development. Many churches do the first two. Very few consistently do the third. Here is a hard truth every church planter must face. If you do not intentionally develop leaders, you will unintentionally limit growth. Small leadership equals small impact. Growing leadership equals a growing church. Multiplying leadership equals multiplying revival. The ceiling of your church will always be the ceiling of your leadership pipeline. Build that pipeline on purpose, or your ceiling will build itself by accident.

The Barnabas Principle

Let me show you the power of leadership development through one of the most overlooked figures in the New Testament: Barnabas. Barnabas never wrote a book of the Bible. He never preached a recorded sermon. He was not one of the original apostles. And yet without Barnabas, Paul may never have been accepted, Mark may never have been restored, and much of the New Testament may never have been written. Barnabas saw what others could not see. When everyone else doubted Saul, Barnabas believed. When Mark failed, Barnabas invested again. He was called the son of encouragement, but do not mistake encouragement for weakness.

Leadership is not about the spotlight. It is about succession, and there is no success without a successor.

Barnabas understood something powerful. Leadership is not about the spotlight. It is about succession. An Apostolic church is built on people who can identify, invest in, and release others. Not control them. Not compete with them. Not compare themselves to them. But develop them. If you want to develop leaders, follow the same mentorship model Jesus used with His disciples. You do, they watch. You do, they help. They do, you help. They do, you watch. He did not just teach them. He involved them. He let them fail in safe places so they could succeed in hard ones. That is how leaders are actually formed.

Overcoming the Fear of Delegation

In the early days of a church plant, almost everything depends on the church planter and their family. That is normal. That is the season. Do not feel guilty about it. But here is the warning. If everything still depends on you after the church is established, you do not have a healthy church. You have a fragile one. A church that cannot function without a single individual is a church that has not been discipled. It has been managed. Managed churches have a ceiling that discipled churches never hit.

There are two reasons church planters fail to develop others even after the church begins to grow. Fear that others will not do it as well. Fear that others might do it better. Both fears are rooted in insecurity. In the early season, carry the weight. That is your assignment. But as God sends people and the church matures, your assignment shifts. Your job is no longer to do everything. Your job is to develop everyone. Share responsibility. Release authority. Celebrate other people's success louder than your own. Your goal is not to be needed forever. Your goal is to build so effectively that your church could thrive even in your absence. That is not a sign of weakness. That is the evidence of real discipleship.

The Hidden Forest

Several years ago, scientists studying forests in remote regions of Canada made a fascinating discovery. The trees in those forests were not competing for survival the way we had always assumed. They were connected. Beneath the surface, an intricate network of roots and fungi allowed trees to share nutrients, send warning signals, and support weaker trees. Even more remarkably, older, stronger trees would send resources to younger, struggling ones. Scientists called these older trees "mother trees." Without them, the forest would not survive.[6]

That is the church. We are not independent. We are interconnected. Mature believers are not just growing for themselves. They are sustaining others. If we fail to disciple, we weaken the entire forest. If we invest in others, we strengthen everything around us. Programs can attract people. Preaching can inspire people. But only discipleship can transform people. And only leadership development can multiply that transformation. A great church is not built by great preaching alone. It is built by ordinary people who are intentionally discipled and then empowered to do the same for somebody else. That is how we change the world, one church at a time.

Discussion & Application

Use these questions for personal reflection or group discussion.

1. Samuel Chand said culture trumps vision. What does your actual culture, not your stated vision, reveal about how your church truly feels toward first-time guests, new converts, and emerging leaders?

2. Who is your one? Name them. What are you currently doing on a weekly basis to pour into that person, and what would have to change in your calendar for that investment to become sustainable?

3. Walk honestly through the three stages: doctrine, distinction, and demonstration. Where do most of the people in your church get stuck, and what is your pastoral responsibility in that stagnation?

4. Think about the difference between consumers and contributors. Which one is your current process producing more of, and what specific step of deployment are you neglecting that keeps developed people from becoming deployed people?

5. Barnabas released Paul, even when it cost him the partnership. Who in your church are you holding too tightly because releasing them would cost you something personally? What would obedience look like this month?

Chapter Fifteen

Developing a Culture of Generosity

S everal years ago, in a remote part of the world, a small village church gathered for a special service. The building was simple. Wooden benches, open windows, a tin roof that echoed every drop of rain. The pastor stood and shared about a need. A neighboring village had no church. No preacher. No witness. They needed help. There was no emotional music. No pressure. No manipulation. Just a simple instruction. "Pray and obey."

After a moment of silence, a woman stood. She was older, frail, and visibly poor. She walked forward holding something in her hands. It was not money. It was her wedding ring. She placed it in the offering. One by one, others followed. A man brought a small tool set, his livelihood. A young boy brought the only shoes he owned. Another family brought a bag of rice that was meant to last the week. By the end of the service, the altar was covered, not with abundance, but with sacrifice. Someone later asked the pastor, "How did you raise so much?" He answered, "We did not raise money. We raised faith."

That is generosity. It is not measured by amount. It is measured by surrender. And here is a truth every church planter must settle early in the journey. There is no such thing as a revival church that is not a giving church. Giving is not just a financial principle. It is a spiritual law. Giving releases the blessings of God upon any congregation, any family, any individual. And if you want to build a church that sustains the presence of God, you must build a culture where generosity flows naturally, not under pressure, but under the anointing.

There is no such thing as a revival church that is not a giving church.

Generosity Is a Culture, Not a Campaign

Many churches treat giving like an event. A special offering. A fundraising push. A seasonal emphasis. But generosity cannot be sustained as an event. It must be built as a culture. Culture answers one question. "What do we naturally do here?" In a generous church, people expect to give. They look for opportunities to give. They celebrate giving. In a church that lacks generosity, offerings feel awkward, conversations about money feel uncomfortable, and giving feels like something being taken rather than something being released. You do not build a giving church by asking for money. You build a giving church by shaping perspective.[1]

Do not talk about giving because the church needs money. Talk about giving because the people of the congregation need the blessing. There is a difference, and it is a critical one. Give people opportunities to give often. Never pressure them. Simply ask them to pray and obey. If there is a special opportunity to give, just say, "There are no preconceived ideas about how much we are going to give today. We simply ask you to pray and obey." That removes manipulation. That removes control. Because you are not telling people what to give now. You are teaching them how to hear. And when people hear from God, they do not need to be convinced.

Do not be afraid to talk about money in your new congregation. Only non-givers are offended by the discussion of giving, because givers already understand that giving is not a loss. It is a gain. You do not need to preach a full message on generosity every week. But you do need consistent moments. Take one to two minutes around the offering to share a short Scripture, a brief testimony, or a simple instructional thought about the value and blessing of giving. Over time, those moments do more than inform. They normalize generosity. They shape thinking. They build faith. And they create culture.

The First Decision That Sets the Tone

There is a moment in every church plant that quietly shapes its financial future. It is not the first sermon. It is not the first service. It is the first financial decision. After opening the church bank account, make the first check out to missions. That decision is not about the amount. It is about identity. It declares to your congregation, to the spirit realm, and to yourself. We are not just here to receive. We are here to release. We are not the end of the pipeline. We are part of the flow. And what you do first becomes what you value most.

This leads to one of the most important foundations of generosity. The tithe is not just ten percent. It is the first ten percent. Anyone can give what is left over. But giving first requires faith. It says, "God, I trust You before I see the outcome." Malachi 3:10 gives one of the most unique invitations in all of Scripture. "Bring ye all the tithes into the storehouse, that there may be meat in mine house, and prove me now herewith, saith the Lord of hosts, if I will not open you the windows of heaven, and pour you out a blessing, that there shall not be room enough to receive it." Tithing is not the ceiling of generosity. It is the floor. It is where giving begins, not where it ends.[2]

Pray and Obey

Let me tell you a story that still marks me to this day. When I was pastoring Westchester Church in New York, we held a missions conference. A church planter from the Northeast was with us, along with a church planting executive. I asked the planter to share his needs with our congregation. He needed a baptistry and some chairs. When he sat back down, I asked him the total. He said about six thousand two hundred dollars. So I challenged our people to give that amount.

What scared me is what happened when I sat back down. God spoke to me clearly. "If they do not give it, you and Lorrie have it." We did. It was in a retirement fund. That was about all we had in there, but it was there. While I would not advise anyone to empty their retirement fund, I would also not advise them to disobey the voice of God regarding giving. Our people, who were normally generous, did not give much that night. There was only one explanation. There had been a message in tongues during the service, but no interpretation was given.

When I got home, I received a text from the sister who had given the message in tongues. She had received the interpretation during the service, but God had not released her to give it publicly. The interpretation was this. "Because of your giving, I will bless you not where you are, but where you are going." Nobody had really given that night except my wife and me. And we had no idea that at that very moment, God was working behind the scenes to open the door for us to relocate to Memphis to pastor Faith Apostolic Church. The people had prayed and obeyed. God told them to give nothing. The message was clear. Do not put pressure on people. Just ask them to pray and obey.

Do not put pressure on people. Just ask them to pray and obey. When people hear from God, they do not need to be convinced.

My Two Cents' Worth

Mark 12 gives us one of the most revealing pictures of Jesus in all of Scripture. "And Jesus sat over against the treasury, and beheld how the people cast money into the treasury" (Mark 12:41). He was not preaching. He was not healing. He was not teaching a parable. He was watching the offering. And I believe Jesus still watches as we give our offerings today. He saw the wealthy throw in large amounts. And then He saw a poor widow drop in two mites, nearly nothing by human standards. But He called His disciples over and said, "Verily I say unto you, That this poor widow hath cast more in, than all they which have cast into the treasury: for all they did cast in of their abundance; but she of her want did cast in all that she had, even all her living" (Mark 12:43–44).

That statement did not make sense mathematically. But it made perfect sense spiritually. God does not measure generosity by what is given. He measures it by what is left. The wealthy gave large amounts, but it cost them little. The widow gave almost nothing, but it cost her everything. In the kingdom of God, sacrifice always outweighs surplus. I am not convinced that God always considers the people we call "big givers" to be "big givers." He is looking at something we cannot see. He is looking at the sacrifice behind the seed.

This is where I want to speak directly to church planters. Often, we do not give because we are embarrassed by how little we have to give. I wish there would be a culture change. Instead of being embarrassed by how little we have to give, we should be embarrassed if we did not give at all. It is not how much we give that matters. It is that we give. Generosity is not a financial threshold. It is a spiritual discipline. And the discipline of giving begins in the season when you feel like you have the least to offer.

God does not measure generosity by what is given. He measures it by what is left. Sacrifice always outweighs surplus.

The Windows of Heaven

There are only three places in Scripture where the windows of heaven are mentioned. In Genesis 7:11, God opened the windows of heaven, and the rain fell in abundance. In 2 Kings 7, Elisha proclaimed by the Word of the Lord that the famine was over, and the windows of heaven produced food in abundance. And in Malachi 3:10, God instructs us on how to get Him to open the windows for ourselves through the tithe. Every time the windows of heaven open, they open in response to the Word of the Lord. And every time they open, they produce abundantly. With Noah and at Samaria, God spoke the Word, and the windows opened. In Malachi, He teaches us what to do to get Him to open them for us.

Windows are amazing things. They let in light from another realm. They give access to the environment of another dimension. They offer a view into what is ahead. Sometimes God does not change your situation immediately, but He opens a window so you can see where you are going. He allows a breeze from a better tomorrow to blow into your today. He raises a window in your spirit, and for the first time in a long time, you can see your future. Paul wrote, "Eye hath not seen, nor ear heard, neither have entered into the heart of man, the things which God hath prepared for them that love him. But God hath revealed them unto us by his Spirit" (1 Corinthians 2:9–10). Giving positions your life under an open heaven.[3]

You Cannot Take It With You, but You Can Send It Ahead

Jesus told a story in Matthew 13:44 that captures the joy of Kingdom investment. "Again, the kingdom of heaven is like unto treasure hid in a field; the which when a man hath found, he hideth, and for joy thereof goeth and selleth all that he hath, and buyeth that field." Notice the phrase "for joy." He did not give reluctantly. He gave joyfully. Because he understood what he was gaining. When you understand what you gain, you stop focusing on what you give. That is the secret to cheerful giving.[4]

Jesus said, "Lay not up for yourselves treasures upon earth, where moth and rust doth corrupt, and where thieves break through and steal: but lay up for yourselves treasures in heaven" (Matthew 6:19–20). He did not say stop storing up treasure. He said stop storing it in the wrong place. You will never see a hearse pulling a U-Haul. You cannot take it with you. But Jesus adds a stunning qualification. By instructing us to lay up treasure in heaven, He is saying you can send it on ahead. Giving is the transfer of temporary wealth into an eternal account that never loses value.

Imagine living in the South during the Civil War. You are a Northerner. You know the war is ending, and Confederate currency is about to become worthless. What would you do?

You would immediately exchange every Confederate dollar for U.S. currency. Now apply that spiritually. Everything on this earth has an expiration date. It will be lost, stolen, or left behind. Jesus gives us the ultimate financial strategy. Transfer your treasure to heaven. This is not the prosperity gospel. This is deferred gratification with an eternal return. Jesus promised that those who sacrifice on earth will receive a hundredfold in return. That is ten thousand percent. No earthly investment will ever match it.

Every Church Has Giving Buckets

It is very important for you to understand that every congregation has giving buckets. Tithe. Offering. Missions. Building fund. There may be others. One of the biggest misconceptions pastors have is this. "If I emphasize missions, it will take away from the tithe." Generosity is not a limited resource. It expands when it is exercised. You need to teach that nothing should take the place of the tithe and offering. That goes to God first. But once you have taught that, you need to understand that those buckets are standalone. What is designated for missions goes only to missions. It does not come from the building fund. It does not come from the tithe and offering. If you never present the opportunity, those funds simply go unaccessed. You are not protecting people by withholding opportunities. You are limiting their obedience. And limited obedience produces limited blessing.

Those Who Gave and Never Lost

R.G. LeTourneau became one of the largest manufacturers of earth-moving equipment in the world. He started by tithing ten percent. Then he gave twenty. Then fifty. Eventually, he lived on ten percent and gave away ninety percent. He famously said, "I shovel it out, and God shovels it back, but God has a bigger shovel." His business did not shrink. It expanded. John Wesley took a different approach. He fixed his standard of living and increased his giving. When his income multiplied, his lifestyle did not change. His giving did. Wesley said, "Earn all you can, save all you can, give all you can."[5]

George Müller ran orphanages for thousands of children without ever asking a single person for money. He only prayed. One morning, there was no food. The children sat at empty tables. Müller prayed and thanked God anyway. Moments later, a baker arrived with fresh bread, and a milk cart broke down outside the orphanage, and the driver donated the entire supply. William Colgate was told as a young man with nothing, "Honor God with your tithe, even when you have nothing." He obeyed. His company became one of the most recognized brands in the world. Different men. Different eras. Different industries. Same principle. They did not wait until they had more to give. They gave, and then God gave more.

What You Release Determines What God Multiplies

In John 6, a crowd of thousands gathered. Hungry. Waiting. Needing a miracle. The disciples saw impossibility. Jesus saw potential. And then a boy stepped forward with five loaves and two fish. It was not enough. It was not even close. But he released it anyway. Jesus took it. Blessed it. Broke it. Multiplied it. And it fed thousands. What if the boy had held on to his lunch? No miracle. No multiplication. No testimony. That is the principle. What you keep, God cannot multiply. What you release, God can bless. That boy did not have abundance. He had just enough. And he opened his hand anyway. Because God has never needed abundance to perform a miracle. He has only ever needed a willing hand.

During World War II, a German businessman named Oskar Schindler owned factories in Nazi-occupied Poland. As the Holocaust unfolded around him, Schindler made a decision that would cost him everything he had. He began using his personal fortune to bribe Nazi officials, falsify records, and employ Jewish workers in his factories, not because he needed their labor, but because his factory floor was the only place they were safe from the death camps. Over the course of the war, Schindler spent every dollar he had. He sold possessions. He emptied accounts. He leveraged relationships. By the time the war ended, he had saved more than eleven hundred Jewish men, women, and children from certain death.

But when the moment came for those survivors to thank him, Schindler did not celebrate. He wept. He looked at his car and said, "This could have saved ten more people." He held up a small gold pin on his lapel and said, "This could have saved two more." He was not grieving what he gave. He was grieving what he kept. At the end of your life, you will not regret what you released for the Kingdom. You will regret what you held back. C.T. Studd inherited a fortune and gave it all away for the sake of the gospel. He wrote words that still echo across the centuries. "Only one life, 'twill soon be past. Only what's done for Christ will last."

What you keep, God cannot multiply. What you release, God can bless. A generous church is not built on wealthy people. It is built on willing people.

So here is the bottom line. Generosity is not about amount. It is about obedience. Giving is not about loss. It is about investment. Tithing is not the finish line. It is the starting point. Pressure does not produce generosity. Faith does. And leadership sets the tone for everything. Model it personally. Teach it consistently. Present opportunities freely. And trust God with the results. A generous church is not built on wealthy people. It is built on willing people. And when people become willing, God does what only He can do. You will never out-give God. So open your hand, church planter. Release what He has placed in your palm. And watch the windows of heaven open over the church He is building through you.[6]

Discussion & Application

Use these questions for personal reflection or group discussion.

1. Is generosity currently a stated value in your church, or is it truly embedded in the culture? How would a first-time guest experience the difference, and what would need to change for generosity to become the atmosphere rather than the announcement?

2. When was the last time you personally gave something that genuinely cost you, and how did that act of sacrifice shape your faith and your leadership? If you cannot point to a recent example, what does that reveal about the ceiling you may be placing on your congregation's generosity?

3. You were told to "pray and obey" rather than pressure. How comfortable are you with the silence that follows that instruction when the offering plate comes back lighter than you hoped? What would it take for you to trust God's voice to your people as much as you trust your own?

4. Look at your church's giving buckets: tithe, offering, missions, and building. Which bucket are you most reluctant to present to your congregation, and is that reluctance based on wisdom or on fear of what they might think?

5. Jesus watched how people gave, not how much. If He sat in your service this Sunday and observed the offering, what would He see in the hearts of your people, and what would He see in yours?

Chapter Sixteen

Loving the Place God Gave You

In 1906, a Norwegian explorer named Helge Ingstad wandered into a forgotten fishing village on the coast of Greenland. The place had been written off. Trade routes had shifted. Harsh winters had chased most families away. What remained was wind, ice, and a handful of stubborn souls who refused to leave. Ingstad asked one elderly man, "Why didn't you leave when everyone else did?" The old man stared across the frozen water and answered, "Because this place knows my name."

That answer never left him. Notice the wording. He did not say, "I know this place." He said, "This place knows me." There is a world of difference between those two sentences. Some people visit places. Others are known by them. That is the gap between a tourist and a missionary. That is the gap between a preacher and a planter. That is the gap between calling and covenant.

If you are going to plant a church, you must settle something early. Will you simply preach in a place, or will you become a part of that place?

Calling Has an Address

We often talk about calling in terms of what God asks us to do. "I'm called to preach." "I'm called to plant." "I'm called to reach people." But Scripture almost never separates calling from geography. When God called Abraham, He did not just hand him a purpose. He handed him a place. "Get thee out of thy country... unto a land that I will shew thee"

(Genesis 12:1).

Calling is not only what. Calling is also where. Daniel Grothe writes that the Christian life is practiced in particular places with particular people.[1] That single sentence cuts against the grain of modern culture. We live in a restless age of mobility and endless options. We are conditioned to believe significance lives somewhere else. A bigger city. A better church. A more strategic location. But the Kingdom of God does not operate on the myth of somewhere better. It operates on the principle of faithfulness right where you are planted.

Calling is not only what. Calling is also where. And the 'where' is never incidental to the will of God.

One of the greatest threats to church planting is not opposition. It is not a lack of resources. It is not even failure. It is emotional transience. That is living in a place physically while remaining uncommitted spiritually.

Charles Kraft's research uncovered a truth every planter needs tattooed on their heart. He found a direct link between a pastor's commitment to a place and spiritual authority in that place.[2] Let that settle down into your bones. Authority is not simply birthed out of gifting. Authority is not simply birthed out of calling. Authority is birthed out of commitment. Kraft described pastors who lived with their emotional and spiritual bags packed, always eyeing the next opportunity. The result was shallow roots and minimal impact. Heaven will not empower what you refuse to own.

You will never have authority over a place you are not willing to stay in. Write that on the inside of your eyelids.

The Covenant That Releases Authority

T. F. Tenney preached a message titled "Power Follows Passion." He reminded us that heaven does not respond to convenience. Heaven responds to hunger. But there is another layer tucked underneath that truth. Passion must have a place to root.

It is not enough to be passionate about ministry in general. You must become passionate about a city in particular. You have to move from "I want revival" to "I want revival here." You have to move from "I love people" to "I love these people." You have to move from

"I'm called to preach" to "I'm called to this city." You must make a covenant with the land. You do not just minister in a place. You bind yourself to it in prayer, in burden, and in longevity. You make a holy decision. "I am not here temporarily. I am here until God gives me a harvest."

Revival does not come to those who date cities. Revival comes to those who marry them.

This is not just theory for me. It is personal. My grandfather, Robert Burchyett, pastored in Cairo, Illinois. Cairo is not the kind of city most people dream about. Once, it carried the promise of becoming a great American city. Its location at the junction of two mighty rivers gave it strategic weight. But over the decades, it suffered one of the most dramatic declines in the country. Businesses packed up. The population crashed. Whole sections of the city were abandoned.

Most folks saw Cairo as a place to leave. My grandfather saw it as a place to love. He believed in Cairo. He talked about Cairo. He invested his life in Cairo. Because one man refused to treat that city as temporary, people heard the gospel there. People were baptized in Jesus' name there. People received the Holy Ghost there. People learned to walk an Apostolic life there. That is the power of loving a place others have given up on.

Frederick Buechner wrote that the place God calls you to is where your deep gladness and the world's deep hunger meet.[3] We usually hear that individually. My gladness. My calling. But Buechner ties vocation to geography. A place. A people. A context. Your calling is not floating in abstraction. It is anchored in an address. Grothe presses further, insisting that sometimes the most significant thing you can do is stay, for the long haul, giving your life away for the good of these people in this place.[4]

That cuts against our instincts. Staying costs something. Staying means working through conflict instead of escaping it. Staying means building relationships rather than replacing them. Staying means believing in a place when nobody else does. Here is the kingdom paradox. Depth only comes through staying. You can travel wide, or you can grow deep. You cannot do both at the same time.

One of the most quietly powerful insights in Grothe's writing is his emphasis on a single word. Just the preposition "of." Jesus was not only Jesus. He was Jesus of Nazareth. Nazareth was not impressive. Nazareth was not strategic. Nazareth carried a bad reputation. "Can there any good thing come out of Nazareth?" (John 1:46). Yet Jesus chose to be identified with that little town. He submitted Himself to a geography. He embraced the limitations of a location. If Jesus was willing to be of a place, who are we to refuse?

G. A. Mangun once said he would sooner leave his wife than leave Alexandria, Louisiana. That is a startling sentence. But it reveals a sacred truth. He did not simply pastor in Alexandria. He was joined to Alexandria. There was a covenant in his bones. Too many planters treat cities like dating relationships. "If it works out, I'll stay." "If it gets hard, I'll leave." "If something better comes along, I'll consider it." But marriage means commitment over convenience. Marriage means covenant over conditions. Marriage means staying power over emotional weather. Your level of commitment to a place will determine your level of authority in that place.

Walls of Wonder and the Cost of Staying

G. K. Chesterton once described children playing on a grassy plateau high above the sea. As long as a wall stood around the edge, the children ran free. They laughed. They shouted. They played right up to the boundaries without a shred of fear. Then someone tore the wall down. Nothing else changed. Same grass. Same sky. Same children. But everything was different. The children stopped running. They stopped laughing. They huddled in the center, afraid to get too close to the edge.[5]

Chesterton's point was profound. Boundaries do not restrict joy. Boundaries create it. Grothe calls them walls of wonder rather than walls of confinement.[6] For the church planter, this matters more than you know. Your city, your region, your assignment is one of those walls. It is not a restriction. It is a protection.

We live in a culture addicted to elsewhere. Elsewhere is always better. A better city. A better opportunity. A better church. A better situation. But elsewhere is often an illusion. It promises significance, yet rarely delivers depth. A long-term study from the American Psychological Association tracked frequent movers and found higher stress, lower relational stability, and decreased well-being.[7] What our culture celebrates as freedom often produces fracture. What Scripture calls stability produces strength. You cannot build deep, life-changing ministry on shallow, transient roots.

You cannot reap from a field you refuse to stay in. Harvest is not random. Harvest is relational.

Throughout Scripture, God consistently ties His work to geography. When God spoke to Abraham, He said, "Arise, walk through the land in the length of it and in the breadth of it; for I will give it unto thee" (Genesis 13:17). God did not tell him to think about the land. He told him to walk it. Possession comes through presence. You do not possess what you will not walk, and you will not walk what you are not committed to.

When famine hit, Isaac had every reason to leave. It would have been logical. It would have been strategic. But God said, "Go not down into Egypt; dwell in the land which I shall tell thee of" (Genesis 26:2). Stay. Not because it was easy, but because it was assigned. And Isaac sowed in famine and reaped a hundredfold. That kind of harvest is not the fruit of perfect conditions. It is the fruit of perfect obedience.

Jacob had an encounter with God at Bethel. It could have been just another night on the run. Instead, he marked the spot. He set up a stone. He poured oil. He named it the house of God. A moment became a marker. A location became sacred. When God meets you somewhere, that place is never just a place again.

Then there was Caleb. Forty-five long years, he carried the same promise. Same land. Same mountain. When the time finally came, he did not ask for something new. He said, "Now therefore give me this mountain, whereof the LORD spake in that day" (Joshua 14:12). Not another opportunity. Not an easier assignment. This one. Covenant does not expire with time.

In the Old Testament, the land was never neutral. Sin defiled it. Obedience blessed it. Repentance healed it. The land vomited out its inhabitants when they turned to wickedness (Leviticus 18). The land was healed when God's people humbled themselves and prayed (2 Chronicles 7:14). Your city is not merely a location. It is an environment that responds to what happens in it. More specifically, it responds to who stays and who leaves.

Authority is the byproduct of proven commitment over time. You do not gain authority in a city in six months. You do not gain authority in a region through occasional effort. Covenant produces consistency. Consistency produces credibility. Credibility produces authority. And authority produces harvest.

Let me be honest with you. Staying is hard. It sounds romantic in theory, but it is grueling in reality. Staying means preaching to the same people when nothing seems to change. Staying means praying when the heavens feel like brass. Staying means building when resources are meager. Staying means loving people who do not always love you back. Grothe tells the story of a pastor named Bob who originally saw his church as a stepping stone. Everything changed when God asked him a single question. "What is your commitment to this place?"[8] That question changed his ministry forever. He realized he could never bring real transformation while living with one foot out the door.

At some point, every church planter has to cross an invisible line. You move from "I'm here to see if this works" to "I am here no matter what." You move from "This is a season" to "This is my assignment." You move from "This is where I am" to "This is who I am of." That shift is not external. It is internal. Once it happens, everything changes. Your preaching gets personal. Your prayers get specific. Your relationships deepen. Your endurance strengthens. You are no longer visiting. You are rooted.

When the Place Becomes an Altar

In 1945, as World War II wound down, a small pocket of Japanese soldiers remained hidden in the jungles of the Philippines. One of them, Hiroo Onoda, refused to surrender for nearly thirty years. Because he believed he was still assigned to that place. Orders had been given. A mission had been entrusted. Even when the world around him shifted, he refused to abandon his post.

History may debate the wisdom of his actions. History cannot deny the power of his commitment. He was not casually connected to that jungle. He was bound to it. Here is what arrests me about that story. He stayed because of a man's command. How much more faithful should we be when our assignment comes from God?

There is a tension we must hold carefully. On one hand, we are called to covenant with the land. On the other hand, God always reserves the prerogative to redirect us. This is where maturity is required. True commitment is not stubbornness. True commitment includes surrender. Sometimes the greatest test of your love for a place is your willingness to lay it on the altar.

You cannot offer something you were never committed to. The altar only has meaning when the covenant was real.

When Lorrie and I moved to New York, we had every intention of dying there. All I ever wanted was to pastor a church as long as possible and watch it become the strongest

Apostolic congregation it could be. About ten years in, God began to deal with me about relocating. It was a long, painful process. God had to speak more clearly about leaving than He had about coming. In many ways, it felt like abandoning my baby. He had birthed in us a dream to plant Westchester Apostolic Church, and we had done exactly that. Now, like Abraham on top of Mount Moriah, He was asking me to offer my Isaac.

Sometimes God does that. We must always follow His lead. But it should take more clarity to leave a place than it did to arrive there. Your default posture is not mobility. Your default posture is faithfulness. Too many church planters do not leave because God speaks. They leave because it is hard. They leave because it is slow. They leave because it is discouraging. They leave because reality did not match their expectations. If you leave too early, you forfeit something you can never get back. You forfeit the depth that only time can produce.

You cannot microwave a harvest. The land must learn your voice, and you must learn its cry. That takes time. Every planter begins by speaking to a place. Preaching. Praying. Proclaiming. But if you stay long enough, there comes a moment when the place starts speaking back. You begin to discern spiritual patterns. You recognize generational strongholds. You learn when to push and when to wait. That kind of insight cannot be downloaded. It must be developed. And it is only developed by staying.

Commitment alone will not sustain you. You must love the place. Love will sustain what duty cannot. You can endure a place for a season through discipline, but you will only pour out your life through affection. Love changes how you see everything. Limitations start looking like opportunities. Problems start looking like assignments. Obstacles start looking like invitations.

Practically, this means learning the history of your city. Understanding its wounds, not just its demographics. Speaking well of it, even when others criticize it. Investing in relationships beyond your church walls. Refusing to compare it to some imaginary better place. Stop saying, "I'm just here for now." Start saying, "This is home."

There is an old story of a man who inherited a small, unimpressive vineyard. The soil was rocky. The yield was low. His neighbors told him to sell it and move on. For years, he worked that vineyard. He pulled stones. He tended vines. He weathered drought and disappointment. Nothing seemed to change. Then one year, something shifted. The vines began to produce. Slowly at first, then abundantly. Decades later, that vineyard became known for some of the richest fruit in the region. When asked what made the difference, the old man simply said, "I stayed." Not brilliance. Not luck. Not perfect conditions. He stayed.

So do not just preach in your city. Marry it. Do not date the place God has given you. Bind yourself to it. Walk its streets. Pray over its soil. Learn its story. Carry its burdens. Weep for its wounded. When the ground feels like granite, and the harvest feels like a rumor, remember this. God does not bless your options. God blesses your obedience. Revival belongs to the one who refuses to leave.

Discussion & Application

Use these questions for personal reflection or group discussion.

1. Charles Kraft linked a pastor's commitment to a place with spiritual authority in that place. Where are the "packed bags" still sitting in your own heart, and what would it look like to start unpacking them this week?

2. Describe the internal shift required to move from "I'm here to see if this works" to "I am here no matter what." What practical decisions would that shift demand from you and your leadership team over the next year?

3. Covenanting with the land means more than just living in your city. What would it look like for you and your core team to walk your streets, learn your city's wounds, and pray over it in the next ninety days?

4. This chapter warns that many planters leave because ministry is hard, not because God clearly speaks. How can you build accountability around the principle that it should take clearer direction to leave a place than it took to come?

5. Think of one neighborhood, school, or overlooked pocket of your city that most people have written off. What would it cost for your church to love that place the way Robert Burchyett loved Cairo, and what is the first concrete step?

Chapter Seventeen

Loving the People God Sends

In the summer of 1878, yellow fever rolled into Memphis, Tennessee, like a black tide. It came up the river from New Orleans, carried on the wings of mosquitoes nobody yet understood. By August, the first bodies lay in the streets. By September, the city had become a graveyard. Out of a population of nearly forty-seven thousand, more than twenty-five thousand people fled in terror. Trains leaving town were packed shoulder to shoulder. Doctors left. Merchants left. Some ministers even locked their church doors and ran. When death moves into a city, survival instincts take over.

Memphis lost over five thousand souls in a matter of weeks. The devastation was so severe that the city would surrender its charter the following year.[1] But not everyone ran. A small group of Episcopal nuns known as the Sisters of St. Mary refused to leave. Sister Constance had only recently arrived in Memphis from New York. When the fever came, her superiors urged her to evacuate with the others. She refused.

Constance and her companions walked into fever-soaked homes and nursed strangers through the night. They took in orphans at the Canfield Asylum when no one else would come near the building. They washed the dying. They sat with children whose parents had died the day before. Catholic priests like Father Charles Parsons joined them. Black ministers stayed when others fled. A handful of doctors, a few Jewish rabbis, and ordinary believers stood beside them. They did not love from a distance. They loved up close. One by one, the very people caring for the sick began to fall sick themselves. Many of them died. History now calls them the Martyrs of Memphis.

They were not killed by persecution. They were consumed by proximity. They got close enough to broken people that it cost them something. That is the heart of a true church planter. Not someone who builds safely from a distance, but someone who gets close enough to the wounded that it demands a piece of them.

If you are going to reach your city, you cannot love it from across the street.

The Way of Blood

Jesus paints the same picture in Luke 10. A seventeen-mile road ran down from Jerusalem to Jericho through narrow passes and shadowed cliffs. Some have called it the Bloody Way because of the robbers who hid along its path. Everyone who traveled that road understood one thing. If you walked it long enough, you would eventually meet a wounded man. Not might. Would. Jesus was not just telling a story. He was describing ministry. Every church planter is assigned to a road like that, a road where people are stripped of dignity, wounded by sin, and suspended between life and death.

The question is not if you will meet them. The question is what you will do when you do.

The story begins with a lawyer. He stands up and asks, "Master, what shall I do to inherit eternal life?" Jesus sends him back to Scripture. Love God and love your neighbor. But Luke tells us the man was "willing to justify himself." The Greek word *dikaioō* means to declare oneself righteous. He was not looking for transformation. He was looking for limitation. "And who is my neighbor?" Hidden inside that question is a dangerous assumption. Surely there must be boundaries to my responsibility. Surely compassion has a ceiling.

We want to know who qualifies for our compassion. Jesus wants to know how far ours will go.

Elie Wiesel once said the opposite of love is not hatred but indifference. That is exactly what the lawyer was flirting with. He wanted a neat definition that would protect him from inconvenience. Jesus refuses to give him one. Instead, He tells a story, because stories expose what arguments conceal.

"A certain man went down from Jerusalem to Jericho, and fell among thieves." Jesus uses three haunting words. Stripped. Wounded. Half dead. The Greek is raw. *Ekdyō* means stripped naked and exposed. They inflicted *plēgai*, blows that left him broken and bleeding. *Hēmithanēs* means caught between life and death. That is not just one man in a ditch. That is humanity. That is the addict who wants freedom but cannot find the door. That is the single parent drowning in bills and grief. That is the teenager quietly planning her own funeral. These people do not just need instruction. They need intervention.

If you misunderstand people, you will mishandle ministry. If you think they are merely uninformed, you will only teach. If you think they are stubborn, you will push harder. But when you understand they are wounded, something shifts inside you.

Then Jesus introduces two religious men, a priest and a Levite. Both saw the wounded man. Both walked on by. That was not ignorance. That was avoidance. They had theology without compassion. They had knowledge without interruption. Dietrich Bonhoeffer wrote that we must be willing to allow ourselves to be interrupted by God. That is exactly what those two refused.

Compassion Before Power

Then comes the Samaritan. "When he saw him, he had compassion on him." The Greek word is *splagchnizomai*, a gut-level stirring in your inner parts. Not surface sympathy. Something that moves you to act. This is not, "I feel bad for you." This is, "I cannot leave you like this." And ultimately, this is Jesus Himself. We were the wounded ones. He came where we were. He touched what others avoided. He bound up our wounds. Before we are ever sent to love like the Samaritan, we must remember we were first loved by Him.

Joel Urshan tells a story about his great-grandfather, A. D. Urshan, that every planter needs to hear. He had been born in the Middle East, had come to America, and had been filled with the Holy Ghost. Now he was going back to preach the gospel to his own family. In his heart, he was walking toward martyrdom. He had no illusions about what awaited him. So he prayed the prayer most of us would pray. "Lord, give me all nine gifts of the Spirit." It made sense. If you are walking into danger, you want power. You want discernment. You want miracles.

But the Lord interrupted him. "You are praying the wrong prayer." So he tried again. "Then, Lord, at least give me the working of miracles and the discerning of spirits." Again, the Lord answered. "You are still praying the wrong prayer." Finally, humbled and desperate, he asked the only question he had left. "Lord, what should I pray?" The answer came with thunder that still echoes today. "Ask Me for compassion. Because when you have compassion, every gift you need will be there when you need it."

Compassion is not a lesser gift. It is the womb out of which every other gift is born.

This is not just a great story. It is a biblical pattern. Over and over in the Gospels, before Jesus performs a miracle, the text tells us He was moved with compassion. Because compassion is not merely an emotion. It is alignment with the heart of God. It is the moment you begin to feel what He feels. When that happens, the miraculous is never far behind. If you want a ministry of power, you must first cultivate a ministry of compassion.

Church planters are builders by nature. We think in terms of systems, strategy, structure, and scalability. Those things matter. But here is the quiet danger. You can build something that grows without building something that heals. You can create environments that attract people without creating environments that transform them. Because transformation is not the product of excellence alone. Transformation is the product of love applied consistently over time. A church with great systems and little love will draw a crowd. A church with great love will raise the dead.

I heard of a missionary who traveled to a rural African village during a brutal drought. The villagers worshiped the crocodiles in the river as gods. As the water receded, their desperation grew. Just before the missionary arrived, the mothers of that village had thrown their babies to the crocodiles, hoping to appease those gods and beg for rain. When he walked into that grief, no sermon could fix what he was seeing. So he did not preach first. He wept first. He walked among those broken mothers, touched them, and prayed for them. As the love of Jesus poured through him, something began to happen. Withered arms were renewed. Lame legs were healed. Countless miracles occurred. Not because he ran a slick service, but because he embodied Christ.

Bob Goff said it with beautiful simplicity. "Love difficult people. You are one of them."[3] That line strips away every excuse. The very people we struggle to love are often mirrors of our own need for grace. Here is a principle every planter must embrace. Your capacity to love determines your capacity to reach. Not your gifting. Not your personality. Not your leadership skill. Your love. Love is what keeps you patient when growth is slow. Love is what keeps you hopeful when results feel delayed. Love sustains what talent cannot.

So how do you grow in compassion? You pray for it. Not for crowds. Not for platforms. Not even for results. You kneel down and ask the Lord to let you feel what He feels. You slow down enough to see people. Most of the needs around you are not hidden. They are simply missed because you are moving too fast to notice them. You get off the platform and into people's actual lives. Love is rarely communicated just from a pulpit. It is communicated through presence. And you stay long enough for people to believe you are not going anywhere. Trust is the door through which transformation walks, and trust is always paid for with time.

Becoming an Inn Jesus Can Trust

Most sermons on the Good Samaritan stop there. But Jesus does not. Because the Samaritan brings the wounded man somewhere. He brings him to an inn. Suddenly, a second character steps onto the stage. The innkeeper. This is where the story turns from salvation to church planting.

The Greek word for inn is *pandocheíon*. It means "a place that receives all." The word for innkeeper is *pandocheús*, "one who welcomes all." That is not just a building. That is a calling. Jesus is still walking the Jericho road today. He is still finding the broken. And when He finds a house He can trust, He keeps bringing them there.

A group of young ministers once gathered around an elderly bishop who had built a thriving church. They had studied his life. They had seen the fruit. They wanted to know his secret. "Bishop, how do you build a church like this?" They expected systems. They expected strategy. The old man looked at them and said, "Boys, the issue is not how to grow a church like this. You are all smart enough to figure that out. The real issue is whether you can love enough to grow a church like this." That answer reframes everything. People are not built by systems. They are built by love.

Jesus does not just send broken people to impressive churches. He sends them to loving ones.

Let us return to Luke 10. The Samaritan issues a command to the innkeeper. "Take care of him." The Greek word is *epimeléomai*. It means sustained, attentive care. Not occasional attention. Not a surface-level check-in. Patient, intentional, ongoing care. This is where ministry becomes real. Reaching people is exciting. Caring for them is demanding. Caring looks like late-night phone calls, walking someone through failure without shaming them, listening when you are tired, forgiving when you are hurt, and showing up when it is inconvenient. It is the work nobody applauds. It is also the work that actually heals.

Years ago, a young woman walked into a small church plant in Queens, New York, with a plan. After the service, she was going home to end her life. Nobody knew. No announcement was made. She had already settled it in her mind. But on the way in that morning, she was met by Brenda Morris, the wife of a church planter who had moved with her husband Gerald from Texas to plant in that city. Brenda wrapped Fotine in the kind of hug only she could give. That was all. One hug.

Fotine went home that afternoon to carry out her plan. But she hesitated. "I have never been hugged like that in my life," she thought. "I have to go back next Sunday for another hug." And she did. That hug became a doorway. That doorway became a life. Today, she is known as Dr. Fotine Christofides, and she has impacted the kingdom of God across the New York City metro for decades. Not because of a sermon. Not because of a program. Because one woman carried the love of Jesus in her arms.

Daniel Grothe writes movingly of Mother Teresa, who never set out to become a global icon.[4] She simply stepped out of her convent into the Bengal famine, and her heart was broken over one sick person at a time. "Not all of us can do great things," she famously said. "But we can all do small things with great love." That is how every great move of God begins. Not with scale. With love.

From Compassion to Guardianship

There comes a moment in every planter's journey when something shifts. At first, you are reaching people. Then you are helping them. Then, without even realizing it, you are carrying them. Their struggles become your prayers. Their burdens become your concern. Their growth becomes your responsibility. This is the moment you move from compassion to guardianship. Compassion feels something. Guardianship holds something.

Paul writes, "Moreover it is required in stewards, that a man be found faithful" (1 Corinthians 4:2). A steward does not own what he manages, but he is fully responsible for it. That is the tension of ministry. These are not your people, yet you are responsible to care for them as though they were. In John 21, Jesus did not tell Peter to grow his platform or expand his reach. He said, "Feed my sheep." Feed. Care. Guard. The measure of ministry is not how many people you gather. It is how well you care for the ones God sends.

Listen to the promise tucked inside the Samaritan's final words. "Take care of him; and whatsoever thou spendest more, when I come again, I will repay thee" (Luke 10:35). There is weight and provision in that single sentence. The weight is the assignment. The promise is the supply. God never calls you to care for people without committing Himself to funding the cost of that care. You cannot outgive the calling. You cannot outlove His supply.

Ministry will demand everything you have, but you are never expected to manufacture what only heaven can supply. The innkeeper was not asked to produce the silver. He was asked to spend it freely and trust that the Samaritan would settle the bill on the return trip. Every planter must settle that same theology in their heart. If He sends them, He will sustain them. If He entrusts them, He will empower you. Your job is not to ration love. Your job is to release it.

You cannot guard what you refuse to feel. You cannot shepherd what you keep at arm's length.

Make no mistake. This calling will stretch you. It will cost you emotionally, spiritually, and personally. People are not projects. They are layered and often messy. If you are not careful, ministry can harden you. You see enough hurt, and you start to protect yourself. You experience enough disappointment, and you begin to disengage. You care less, so it hurts less. But that is a dangerous place. You cannot guard what you refuse to feel. You cannot build what you are unwilling to carry. If you want to reach people, you must be willing to feel people.

In 1940, during the early days of World War II, thousands of Allied soldiers were trapped on the beaches of Dunkirk. Enemy forces were closing in, and evacuation by naval vessels seemed impossible because the big ships could not get close enough to shore. Then something unexpected happened. Hundreds of small civilian boats, fishing vessels, lifeboats, and personal crafts began crossing the English Channel. Ordinary people with no military training went anyway. They pulled soldiers from the water and lifted them off the sand.[5]

Eyewitness accounts describe the same scene over and over. A little boat already full. Danger pressing in. Time running out. And someone on board would say, "We can take one more." One more soldier. One more life. One more rescue. That is the spirit of a church planter who understands the assignment. Not, "We have done enough," but, "We can take one more." One more broken life. One more hurting family. One more soul that needs hope. Successful church planters do not stop at capacity. They stretch. They sacrifice. They make room.

That is what the Martyrs of Memphis did. That is what Brenda Morris did in Queens. That is what the unnamed missionary did in that African village. That is what A. D. Urshan did in the Middle East. They saw someone the world had written off, and they said, "We can take one more." Heaven has always moved through people willing to carry one more name, one more burden, one more broken soul. The ones God remembers are rarely the ones with the biggest platforms. They are the ones with the biggest hearts.

The Samaritan is still walking the road. He is still asking the same question of every church planter and every congregation. "Can I trust this house with the hurting?" If He finds an open door, a compassionate spirit, and a committed innkeeper, He will keep bringing the broken. And He will cover every cost.

Discussion & Application

Use these questions for personal reflection or group discussion.

1. The Martyrs of Memphis died because they got close enough to suffering to be touched by it. Where in your ministry are you tempted to love from a safe distance, and what would true proximity cost you this month?

2. A. D. Urshan kept praying for gifts until God redirected him toward compassion. If God audited your prayer life as a planter, what would He say you are asking for most, and what prayer is He inviting you into instead?

3. The Greek word *epimeléomai* means sustained, attentive care. Identify one person in your church who needs that kind of care right now. What would a six-month plan of that kind of care look like for them?

4. The elder bishop said the real question is not how to grow a church but whether you can love enough to grow one. What concrete habits can you and your leadership team build this year to expand your capacity to love difficult people?

5. Successful church planters say, "We can take one more." Where is your church at capacity emotionally, spiritually, or structurally, and where is the Holy Ghost asking you to stretch and make room for one more?

Chapter Eighteen

Give Me This Mountain

In September of 1862, during the American Civil War, a Union soldier named Barton Mitchell was walking through a field near Frederick, Maryland. He noticed something lying in the grass. It did not look like much. Just a small bundle. Three cigars wrapped in paper. Curious, he picked it up. Inside that paper were battle plans. Detailed orders from Confederate General Robert E. Lee outlining troop movements and strategy. It was called Special Order 191. The plans had been lost, forgotten, dropped by accident. When they were discovered, everything changed.

Union General George McClellan now knew where the enemy was, how they were positioned, and what they planned to do next. It gave him an advantage he should have never had. Historians call it one of the greatest intelligence breakthroughs of the war.[1] Yet here is the tragedy. McClellan hesitated. He delayed. He overanalyzed. Instead of decisively defeating Lee's army, he allowed the moment to slip. The opportunity was real. The advantage was clear. But hesitation cost him the victory.

There are moments in life where everything changes. Moments where the opportunity is clear, the calling is undeniable, and the promise is within reach. But the difference between those who step into destiny and those who drift away from it is not opportunity. It is action. McClellan had the plans. He had the advantage. He had the moment. What he lacked was the courage to move. And church planter, you are standing in one of those moments right now. The question is no longer whether God has called you. The question is whether you will step forward or hesitate on your promise.

Let that sink in. The cigars in the grass were not the miracle. The miracle was the willingness to pick them up. And the tragedy was the unwillingness to act on what picking them up revealed. Heaven has already dropped the orders at your feet. Somebody just has to have the courage to read them and move.

Hesitation is the silent killer of calling. The opportunity will not wait on your courage to catch up.

Men Wanted for a Hazardous Journey

Fast forward to 1914. Explorer Ernest Shackleton placed an advertisement in a London newspaper recruiting men for an expedition across Antarctica. The ad reportedly read, "Men wanted for hazardous journey. Small wages. Bitter cold. Long months of complete darkness. Constant danger. Safe return doubtful. Honor and recognition in case of success." Most people assumed nobody would respond. They were wrong. Thousands of men applied. Thousands. Because there is something inside the human spirit that still answers a call worth dying for.

Heaven is still running that ad. God is still looking for people who will say yes to a call that offers small wages and bitter resistance. He is looking for church planters who will trade comfort for calling. The impossible is simply where God begins. If the path in front of you looks clear, safe, and predictable, you may not actually be walking in a divine assignment. The call of God has always had danger written on the front of it.

The impossible is simply where God begins.

Shackleton went on to lead one of the most remarkable survival stories in human history. His ship, the Endurance, was crushed by ice in the Weddell Sea in 1915. For nearly two years, he and his men lived on ice floes. Then they sailed a small lifeboat across eight hundred miles of the most treacherous ocean on earth to reach South Georgia Island. Shackleton then hiked across uncharted mountains to reach a whaling station and organize a rescue. Every one of his twenty-eight men survived.[2] All of them. Because one leader refused to quit. Heaven is not short on opportunities. Heaven is short on leaders who will stand up in the middle of the ice and say, "We are getting home."

Why Sit We Here Until We Die?

Second Kings 7 tells the story of four lepers sitting at the gate of Samaria during a brutal famine. The city was starving. The Syrian army was camped outside. The lepers were outcasts, the kind of people nobody expected to become heroes. But one of them spoke up with a sentence that still preaches. "Why sit we here until we die?" They decided to walk into the enemy camp and take their chances. What they did not know was that God had already gone ahead of them. He had caused the Syrians to hear the sound of a great host, and the soldiers fled in terror, leaving food, silver, gold, and clothing behind.[3]

Four disqualified men walked into an empty camp and fed an entire starving city. What feels impossible to you is already settled in the mind of God. The battle you are afraid to fight may already be won. The camp you are afraid to enter may already be empty. You will never know until you rise from the gate and start walking. Church planter, stop sitting at the edge of your assignment asking, "Can I do this?" Start asking, "Why sit I here until I die?"

What feels impossible to you is already settled in the mind of God. The camp you fear to enter may already be empty.

Another Spirit

That brings us to Caleb. Israel stood at Kadesh-barnea, the doorway to the Promised Land. Twelve men went to spy out the territory. Ten came back with fear. Two came back with faith. The ten said, "The walls are too big. The giants are too strong. We look like grasshoppers." Joshua and Caleb declared, "If God is with us, we can take the land." Same land. Same giants. Same moment. Different spirit. Henry Ford once said, "Whether you think you can or you think you can't, you're right." The ten proved him true in the negative. Joshua and Caleb proved him true in the positive.

Historians estimate Israel's population at over two million people at that moment. Joshua and Caleb were literally one in a million. Nobody builds monuments to men who say it cannot be done. History remembers giant slayers, not naysayers. Numbers 14:24 says Caleb "had another spirit with him, and hath followed me fully." That phrase changes everything. Caleb thought differently. He believed differently. He responded differently. Fear says you can't. Faith says you must. The difference between the ten and the two was not information. It was inspiration from another realm.

William Carey, the father of modern missions, said it this way. "Expect great things from God. Attempt great things for God." That is Caleb in a sentence. He expected, and then he attempted. For forty-five years, he carried the vision in his heart before he ever held it in his hands. Through wilderness wandering. Through funerals. Through rejection. But vision lives in the heart long before it shows up in reality. Every church planter understands this. You see the church before it exists. You see the baptisms before the baptistry is installed. You see the revival before the first service.

You may be tempted to compare your mountain to somebody else's. Do not do it. Your mountain was chosen for you. Your assignment was measured for you. Your giants were named for you before you were ever born. Comparison is the quickest way to forfeit a calling. The ten spies compared themselves to the giants and said, "We were in our own sight as grasshoppers, and so we were in their sight." Notice the sequence. They became grasshoppers in their own eyes first. They believed that the enemy saw what they had already decided about themselves. Your self-assessment is always prophetic. What you believe about yourself today is what you think the giants will see tomorrow.

Forty-Five Years Later

Fast forward to Joshua 14. Caleb is eighty-five years old. He walks up to Joshua and says, "I am as strong this day as I was in the day that Moses sent me." Then he speaks the words that have echoed through every generation of bold believers. "Now therefore give me this mountain, whereof the Lord spake in that day." Not the valley. Not the easy place. The mountain. The place where giants still lived, cities were still walled, and the battle was guaranteed. Because the greatest blessings are always fenced by the greatest battles.

Caleb wanted that mountain because it was his promise, because with God he was able, because it was his heritage, and because it was his vision. But here is what makes his story remarkable. Joshua 14:6 calls him "Caleb the son of Jephunneh the Kenizzite." The Kenizzites were a Gentile people. Caleb was not a full-blooded Jew. He was an outsider by birth who chose the people of God, embraced their promise, and followed the Lord with his whole heart.[4] His heritage was not defined by where he came from. It was defined by who he followed.

If God called you, then your limitation is not a liability. It is the stage for His power.

You may not have a Pentecostal pedigree. You may not have the right last name. You may not have come from the right family, the right school, or the right background. But when you were baptized in Jesus' name, you received the only name that matters. The kingdom of God has never been built on pedigree. It has always been built on faith. Joshua 15:14 tells us Caleb drove out three giants. Sheshai, Ahiman, and Talmai. Their names reveal the enemies every leader must conquer. Sheshai, "who I am," the giant of ego. Ahiman, "what I am," the giant of pride. Talmai, "what I can do," the giant of self-reliance. Revival never flows through any of the three.

And do not miss what happened to Othniel, Caleb's nephew. After Caleb conquered the three giants, he made an unusual declaration. He said that whoever conquered Kirjath-sepher would marry his daughter. In other words, "I want my daughter to marry a champion. I want the next generation raised by someone who knows how to fight." Othniel stepped forward, conquered the city, and married Caleb's daughter. Years later, when Israel fell into oppression under a king whose name meant double wickedness, God raised up a deliverer. It was Othniel. Because Caleb valued courage, an entire generation experienced deliverance. What you conquer today becomes what others inherit tomorrow.

Still Growing

In his book The Sower's Seeds, Brian Cavanaugh tells the story of Sir Edmund Hillary, the first man to climb Mount Everest.[5] In 1952, Hillary tried to climb Everest and failed. He had to turn back. A few weeks later, a group in England invited him to speak. When Hillary walked onto the stage, the audience erupted in applause. But he did not feel like a hero. He felt like a failure. Instead of going to the microphone, he walked to the edge of the stage where a large photograph of Mount Everest hung behind him.

He clenched his fist, pointed at the mountain, and said loudly, "Mount Everest, you beat me the first time. But I will beat you the next time, because you have grown all you are going to grow, but I am still growing." One year later, he stood on top of the world. Nelson Mandela put it this way. "It always seems impossible until it is done." The mountain never changed. Hillary did. And that is the spirit of Caleb. Your mountain may not move. But you can grow. And what is still growing will always eventually overtake what has stopped.

Your willingness will take you where your experience never could. Heaven rewards the heart that refuses to stop growing.

A Child of the King

Ben Hooper grew up in difficult circumstances in the hills of East Tennessee. He was born out of wedlock, and the community never let him forget it. People whispered as he walked by. Children on the playground called him names. When he went to the general store, adults would ask the cruel question, "Boy, who's your daddy?" He never had an answer. He grew up ashamed of a question he could not answer. One Sunday, a new preacher came to a little church in the area, and young Ben slipped in to hear him. He tried to leave quickly to avoid the usual questions, but the preacher stopped him at the door.

The preacher put his hand on the boy's shoulder, looked straight into his eyes, and said, "Son, I know who you are. I can see the family resemblance. You are a child of the King." Ben Hooper later said, "That was the day I was elected the governor of Tennessee." Of course, it took him years to grow up and run for office. But that little boy grew up to become the governor of Tennessee. One sentence from a preacher who saw his true identity changed the entire trajectory of his life. Your identity is not determined by your past, your background, or your limitations. It is determined by your calling. And children of the King take mountains.

Let me say something to the church planter who is tired. Who has been climbing a mountain that refuses to shrink. Who is watching other ministries grow while yours feels stuck. Hear me clearly. The mountain is not the enemy. Stagnation is. As long as you keep growing, you have not lost. Hillary lost on Everest in 1952, but he was not defeated. He was in training. The Spirit of God is not finished with you. The same God who took Caleb from the wilderness to Hebron at age eighty-five is still in the business of honoring those who refuse to let their vision die. Keep growing in prayer. Keep growing in the Word. Keep growing in faith. And watch what God does with a servant who simply refuses to stop.

Only God: The Westchester Story

Let me bring this home. What business did two kids from Arkansas have moving to the New York City metro to plant an Apostolic church? None. No connections. No platform. No advantage. We did not have the right accent. We did not have the right résumé. We did not have the right budget. What we had was a call, a promise, and a willingness to go. And God met us on the journey in ways we could never have manufactured. Westchester Apostolic Church was established in November of 2003 with a core group of seven people who could have fit into a minivan.

Today, under the leadership of Donny and Ashley Willis, Westchester Apostolic Church has purchased a permanent building in downtown White Plains, New York. A Spanish-speaking congregation has also been established in White Plains. Another congregation has been launched in Manhattan. Only God. The seven people in the minivan became a movement that continues to multiply. None of that would have happened if two kids from Arkansas had waited until they felt qualified. They never would have gone. They simply said yes, and God did what only God can do.

I want you to understand something about this final chapter of a book on church planting. The man writing these words is not writing from theory. Lorrie and I packed a moving truck in Arkansas. We drove it to Westchester County, New York. We walked into neighborhoods where we knew nobody. We attended street fairs and handed out bottles of water. We sat in coffee shops and taught Bible studies. We wept over a city that did not know us and did not ask us to come. In the middle of all of it, God showed up in ways that still make me shake my head. That is why I can tell you with absolute confidence that if God is speaking to you about a city, a community, or a calling, He will not fail you when you go.

The Final Charge

So we come to the end of this book. Not as a conclusion, but as a commissioning. You have read about the calling, the preparation, the process, and the principles. You have heard about Jamestown settlers, Jeremiah Lanphier's six people, Tom Lee's little boat, Azusa Street, the widow's two mites, and Caleb's mountain. Now comes the only question that actually matters. What will you do with it? Knowledge is not enough. Inspiration is not enough. Even calling is not enough. Action is what matters. The battle plans will not carry themselves to the general. The ad will not answer itself. The gate of Samaria will not walk itself into the empty camp. The mountain will not climb itself.

This is the moment the reading ends and the sending begins. Every page you have turned was not just information. It was preparation. Every story was a witness. Every principle was a promise. Every Scripture was a sword placed carefully in your hand. You are no longer a reader. You are a recruit. And the Commander of heaven's armies is looking straight at you with one question burning in His eyes. "Whom shall I send, and who will go for us?" There is only one right answer. "Here am I. Send me." Caleb did not whisper his request. He declared it. So declare it with me, church planter. Give me my city. Give me my community. Give me my assignment. Give me this mountain. You are called. You are equipped. You are able through Him. The promise is still real. The harvest is still ready. The mountain still belongs to the people of God. So rise. Take the step. Start the work. Trust God. Plant the church. Reach the city. Disciple the nations. And change the world, one church at a time. If the Lord be with you, you shall be able to drive them out, just as the Lord has said. Your mountain is waiting. Go take it.

The book is done. The call is clear. Your mountain is waiting, and heaven is watching. Go.

And let me remind you of one more thing as this book closes. The God who met a shepherd boy in a field, who called a fisherman from his nets, who anointed a Gentile outsider to slay giants, and who used two kids from Arkansas to plant a church in New York is still in the business of writing impossible stories. Your name could be the next one on that list. But only if you are willing to stop hesitating and start obeying. Take the step. Start the work. Trust God. You can do this.

One generation from now, somebody will walk into a church that exists because you obeyed. A mother will find deliverance at an altar you built. A teenager will be filled with the Holy Ghost in a sanctuary you prayed into existence. A broken marriage will be restored in a room you rented, swept, and dedicated to the Lord. A prodigal will come home because you planted a lighthouse in a dark part of town. Your yes matters more than you know. The people who will be reached through your obedience are not yet on your prayer list because you have not met them yet. But heaven has. And heaven is waiting on you to go get them.

So hear this final word from one church planter to another. Stop rehearsing your disqualifications. Stop waiting on the perfect sending service. Stop comparing your calling to somebody else's highlight reel. Stop asking for a shortcut God never promised. Go. The God who called you will meet you on the road. The mountain belongs to the Lord, and the Lord is looking for a servant humble enough to ask for it and bold enough to climb it. Give Him your yes. He will do the rest.

Now receive this benediction over your life and your calling. May the God of Abraham who called him to a land he did not know, the God of Caleb who gave him the mountain he refused to forget, the God of Peter who walked with him on water, and the God of Paul who met him on a dusty road, go before you, walk beside you, and rise up behind you. May He make your house an inn Jesus can trust. May He make your preaching a fire and your prayers a flood. May your children serve Him. May your city know His name. May the church you plant outlive you by a hundred years, and may the last soul it reaches be standing with you on the day Jesus rewards the faithful.

And if anyone ever asks how it all began, tell them the truth. Tell them a church planter heard from God, answered the ad, climbed the mountain, and refused to turn back. Tell them God did the rest. And then hand this book to the next planter in line, because the assignment is not finished until every city has an Apostolic witness. The mountain is yours. The harvest is yours. The moment is yours. Now go, church planter. Go in the name of Jesus. And do not come back until the land is taken.

Discussion & Application

Use these questions for personal reflection or group discussion.

1. The cigars illustration shows that opportunity without action is wasted. What specific opportunity has God placed in your hands that you have been hesitating to act on, and what is hesitation already costing you?

2. Shackleton's recruitment ad promised hardship, not comfort. If God ran a similarly honest ad for your calling, what would it say, and would you still answer it?

3. Caleb carried his vision for forty-five years before he possessed it. What promise has God spoken over your life that you are tempted to let die, and what will you do this week to keep the picture alive in your heart?

4. Examine the three giants: Sheshai (ego), Ahiman (pride), and Talmai (self-reliance). Which one is most active in your heart right now, and how is it hindering the flow of revival through you?

5. If you stood up today and declared, "Give me this mountain," what would have to change in your calendar, your prayer life, your finances, and your courage by this time next month?

Notes

CHAPTER 1. THE ADVENTURE OF A LIFETIME

1. Timothy Keller, *Center Church: Doing Balanced, Gospel-Centered Ministry in Your City* (Grand Rapids: Zondervan, 2012), 355–372.

2. Ed Stetzer and Daniel Im, *Planting Missional Churches: Your Guide to Starting Churches That Multiply*, 2nd ed. (Nashville: B&H Academic, 2016), 14–18.

3. Henry T. Blackaby and Richard Blackaby, *Spiritual Leadership: Moving People on to God's Agenda*, rev. ed. (Nashville: B&H Publishing Group, 2011), 42–45.

4. Craig Groeschel, *It: How Churches and Leaders Can Get It and Keep It* (Grand Rapids: Zondervan, 2008), 178–183.

5. Assemblies of the Lord Jesus Christ (~400 churches), Worldwide Pentecostal Fellowship (~265 churches), United Pentecostal Church International (~5,200 churches).

6. Eckhard J. Schnabel, *Early Christian Mission*, vol. 2, *Paul and the Early Church* (Downers Grove, IL: InterVarsity Press, 2021), 1222–1240.

CHAPTER 2. WHEN A CITY GETS IN YOUR SPIRIT

1. Christopher J. H. Wright, *The Mission of God: Unlocking the Bible's Grand Narrative* (Downers Grove, IL: IVP Academic, 2005), 189–215.

2. Carey Nieuwhof, *Didn't See It Coming: Overcoming the Seven Greatest Challenges That No One Expects and Everyone Experiences* (New York: WaterBrook, 2018), 63–68.

3. Henry T. Blackaby and Richard Blackaby, *Spiritual Leadership: Moving People on to

God's Agenda, rev. ed. (Nashville: B&H Publishing Group, 2011), 27–32.

4. J. D. Greear, *Gaining by Losing: Why the Future Belongs to Churches That Send* (Grand Rapids: Zondervan, 2015), 88–95.

5. Robert E. Coleman, *The Master Plan of Evangelism*, 2nd ed. (Grand Rapids: Revell, 2019), 21–27.

CHAPTER 3. SOMEONE HAS TO RESPOND

1. Bibb Latané and John M. Darley, *The Unresponsive Bystander: Why Doesn't He Help?* (New York: Appleton-Century-Crofts, 1970), 31–45.

2. John Maxwell, *The 21 Irrefutable Laws of Leadership: Follow Them and People Will Follow You*, rev. ed. (Nashville: Thomas Nelson, 2007), 143–152.

3. Timothy Keller, *Center Church: Doing Balanced, Gospel-Centered Ministry in Your City* (Grand Rapids: Zondervan, 2012), 355–365.

4. Henry T. Blackaby and Claude V. King, *Experiencing God: Knowing and Doing the Will of God*, rev. ed. (Nashville: B&H Publishing Group, 2004), 138–145.

5. Robert E. Coleman, *The Master Plan of Evangelism*, 2nd ed. (Grand Rapids: Revell, 2019), 21–27.

6. Thom S. Rainer and Eric Geiger, *Simple Church: Returning to God's Process for Making Disciples*, rev. ed. (Nashville: B&H Publishing Group, 2011), 67–74.

CHAPTER 4. PREPARING THE CHURCH PLANTER

1. David McCullough, *The Wright Brothers* (New York: Simon & Schuster, 2016), 45–72.

2. F. F. Bruce, *Paul: Apostle of the Heart Set Free* (Grand Rapids: Eerdmans, 2000), 81–95.

3. John C. Maxwell, *The 21 Irrefutable Laws of Leadership: Follow Them and People Will Follow You*, rev. ed. (Nashville: Thomas Nelson, 2007), 23–27.

4. Henry Cloud, *Integrity: The Courage to Meet the Demands of Reality* (New York: HarperCollins, 2006), 119–136.

5. Dave Ramsey, *The Total Money Makeover: A Proven Plan for Financial Fitness*, rev. ed. (Nashville: Thomas Nelson, 2009), 21–35.

6. Henry T. Blackaby and Richard Blackaby, *Spiritual Leadership: Moving People on to God's Agenda*, rev. ed. (Nashville: B&H Publishing Group, 2011), 115–128.

7. Mark Batterson, *The Circle Maker: Praying Circles Around Your Biggest Dreams and Greatest Fears* (Grand Rapids: Zondervan, 2016), 17–23.

CHAPTER 5. STAYING CONNECTED TO THE SOURCE

1. Mark Batterson, *The Circle Maker: Praying Circles Around Your Biggest Dreams and Greatest Fears* (Grand Rapids: Zondervan, 2016), 17–23.

2. Henry T. Blackaby and Richard Blackaby, *Spiritual Leadership: Moving People on to God's Agenda*, rev. ed. (Nashville: B&H Publishing Group, 2011), 148–155.

3. John Knox, quoted in Thomas M'Crie, *The Life of John Knox* (Edinburgh: Blackwood, 1812), 274.

4. M'Crie, *The Life of John Knox*, 281.

5. Jennifer Hooper McCarty and Tim Foecke, *What Really Sank the Titanic: New Forensic Discoveries* (New York: Citadel Press, 2008), 112–128.

CHAPTER 6. CHOOSE LIFE

1. Humphrey Carpenter, *J. R. R. Tolkien: A Biography* (New York: HarperCollins, 2016), 99–123.

2. Willem A. VanGemeren, ed., *New International Dictionary of Old Testament Theology and Exegesis*, vol. 2 (Grand Rapids: Zondervan, 1997), 935–937.

3. Walter Bauer, *A Greek-English Lexicon of the New Testament and Other Early Christian Literature*, 3rd ed. (Chicago: University of Chicago Press, 2001), 622–623.

4. Ceslas Spicq, *Theological Lexicon of the New Testament*, vol. 1 (Peabody, MA: Hendrickson, 2023), 355–356.

5. Neal Gabler, *Walt Disney: The Triumph of the American Imagination* (New York:

Vintage Books, 2007), 676.

CHAPTER 7. BLESS ME INDEED

1. Eifion Evans, *The Welsh Revival of 1904* (Bridgend, Wales: Evangelical Press of Wales, 1974), 70–85.

2. Howard Taylor, *Hudson Taylor's Spiritual Secret* (Chicago: Moody Publishers, 2009), 112.

3. John Maxwell, *The 21 Irrefutable Laws of Leadership: Follow Them and People Will Follow You*, rev. ed. (Nashville: Thomas Nelson, 2007), 267.

4. Edith L. Blumhofer, *Her Heart Can See: The Life and Hymns of Fanny J. Crosby* (Grand Rapids: Eerdmans, 2005), 3–15.

5. A. W. Tozer, *The Pursuit of God* (Chicago: Moody Publishers, 2015), 17.

6. F. B. Meyer, *The Secret of Guidance* (Chicago: Moody Press, 2010), 58.

7. Dallas Willard, *The Great Omission: Reclaiming Jesus's Essential Teachings on Discipleship* (New York: HarperOne, 2006), xi.

8. Bill Hybels, *Courageous Leadership* (Grand Rapids: Zondervan, 2002), 185.

CHAPTER 8. THE LIFE GOD BLESSES

1. Henry T. Blackaby and Richard Blackaby, *Spiritual Leadership: Moving People on to God's Agenda*, rev. ed. (Nashville: B&H Publishing Group, 2011), 120–128.

2. Dietrich Bonhoeffer, *The Cost of Discipleship* (New York: Touchstone, 1995), 105–107.

3. D. Martyn Lloyd-Jones, *Studies in the Sermon on the Mount* (Grand Rapids: Eerdmans, 1971), 68–70.

4. Dallas Willard, *The Spirit of the Disciplines: Understanding How God Changes Lives* (San Francisco: HarperCollins, 1988), 156–163.

CHAPTER 9. THE FIRST CHURCH YOU PLANT

1. James C. Dobson, *Bringing Up Boys: Practical Advice and Encouragement for Those Shaping the Next Generation of Men* (Carol Stream, IL: Tyndale House, 2001), 55–58.

2. Daniel Grothe, *The Power of Place: Choosing Stability in a Rootless Age* (Nashville: Thomas Nelson, 2021), 148–149.

3. Grothe, *The Power of Place*, 139–140.

4. Grothe, *The Power of Place*, 152.

5. Grothe, *The Power of Place*, 81.

6. Gary Smalley and John Trent, *The Blessing: Giving the Gift of Unconditional Love and Acceptance* (Nashville: Thomas Nelson, 2019), 27.

7. Lewis B. Smedes, *Forgive and Forget: Healing the Hurts We Don't Deserve* (San Francisco: HarperOne, 1984), 133.

8. R. Kent Hughes, *Disciplines of a Godly Man* (Wheaton, IL: Crossway, 2012), 33–34.

CHAPTER 10. BUILT TO STAND TOGETHER

1. Richard Preston, *The Wild Trees: A Story of Passion and Daring* (New York: Random House, 2007), 22–24.

2. John C. Maxwell, *The 17 Indisputable Laws of Teamwork* (Nashville: Thomas Nelson, 2001), 3–5.

3. E. M. Bounds, *Power Through Prayer* (Grand Rapids: Baker Books, 1972), 11–14.

4. J. D. Payne, *Discovering Church Planting: An Introduction to the Whats, Whys, and Hows of Global Church Planting* (Downers Grove, IL: IVP, 2009), 217–220.

5. Hudson Taylor, *Hudson Taylor's Spiritual Secret* (Chicago: Moody Publishers, 2009), 43.

6. Ed Stetzer and Daniel Im, *Planting Missional Churches: Your Guide to Starting Churches That Multiply, 2nd ed.* (Nashville: B&H Academic, 2016), 67–82.

7. Charles Fishman, *One Giant Leap: The Impossible Mission That Flew Us to the Moon* (New York: Simon & Schuster, 2019), 1–6.

CHAPTER 11. FIRST THINGS FIRST

1. James Horn, *A Land as God Made It: Jamestown and the Birth of America* (New York: Basic Books, 2005), 154–162.

2. Gordon MacDonald, *Ordering Your Private World, rev. ed.* (Nashville: Thomas Nelson, 2003), 23–31.

3. Peter Scazzero, *The Emotionally Healthy Leader* (Grand Rapids: Zondervan, 2015), 45–58.

4. Richard A. Swenson, *Margin: Restoring Emotional, Physical, Financial, and Time Reserves to Overloaded Lives* (Colorado Springs: NavPress, 2004), 69–78.

5. J. I. Packer, *A Passion for Faithfulness: Wisdom from the Book of Nehemiah* (Wheaton, IL: Crossway, 1995), 54–67.

6. John C. Maxwell, *Everyone Communicates, Few Connect: What the Most Effective People Do Differently* (Nashville: Thomas Nelson, 2010), 3–15.

7. Ed Stetzer and Daniel Im, *Planting Missional Churches: Your Guide to Starting Churches That Multiply, 2nd ed.* (Nashville: B&H Academic, 2016), 189–202.

8. Alan Hirsch, *The Forgotten Ways: Reactivating Apostolic Movements, 2nd ed.* (Grand Rapids: Brazos Press, 2016), 217–229.

9. Robert E. Coleman, *The Master Plan of Evangelism, rev. ed.* (Grand Rapids: Revell, 2019), 41–54.

CHAPTER 12. FROM TABLE TO TRANSFORMATION

1. John E. Harkins, *Memphis Chronicles: Bits of History from the Best Times Magazine* (Charleston, SC: The History Press, 2009), 78–85.

2. Craig S. Keener, *The Gospel of John: A Commentary, vol. 1* (Grand Rapids: Baker Academic, 2010), 737–742.

3. Randy Newman, *Questioning Evangelism: Engaging People's Hearts the Way Jesus Did,* 2nd ed. (Grand Rapids: Kregel, 2017), 27–39.

4. Robert E. Coleman, *The Master Plan of Evangelism, rev. ed.* (Grand Rapids: Revell, 2019), 41–54.

5. Alan Hirsch, *The Forgotten Ways: Reactivating Apostolic Movements, 2nd ed.* (Grand Rapids: Brazos Press, 2016), 217–229.

6. Jerry O. Potter, *The Sultana Tragedy: America's Greatest Maritime Disaster* (Gretna, LA: Pelican Publishing, 1992), 87–104.

CHAPTER 13. THE FIRST SERVICE

1. J. Edwin Orr, *The Event of the Century: The 1857–1858 Awakening* (Wheaton, IL: Richard Owen Roberts Publishing, 1989), 17–34.

2. Aubrey Malphurs, *Planting Growing Churches for the 21st Century: A Comprehensive Guide for New Churches and Those Desiring Renewal, 4th ed.* (Grand Rapids: Baker Books, 1998), 248–262.

3. Richard R. Hammar, *Pastor, Church & Law, 5th ed., vol. 1* (Carol Stream, IL: Christianity Today, 2019), 91–118.

4. Francis Chan, *Letters to the Church* (Colorado Springs: David C. Cook, 2018), 73–88.

5. Andy Stanley, *Deep and Wide: Creating Churches Unchurched People Love to Attend, 2nd ed.* (Grand Rapids: Zondervan, 2016), 201–215.

6. Frank Bartleman, *Azusa Street: The Roots of Modern-Day Pentecost* (Plainfield, NJ: Logos International, 1980), 43–58.

CHAPTER 14. DEVELOPING A CULTURE OF DISCIPLESHIP

1. Samuel R. Chand, *Cracking Your Church's Culture Code: Seven Keys to Unleashing Vision and Inspiration* (San Francisco: Jossey-Bass, 2010), 1–15.

2. Dallas Willard, *The Great Omission: Reclaiming Jesus's Essential Teachings on Discipleship* (New York: HarperOne, 2006), 3–15.

3. Dietrich Bonhoeffer, *The Cost of Discipleship, rev. ed.* (New York: Touchstone, 1995), 43–56.

4. Stan O. Gleason, *Follow To Lead: The Journey of a Disciple Maker* (Weldon Spring, MO: Word Aflame Press, 2016), 59–60.

5. Robert E. Coleman, *The Master Plan of Evangelism, rev. ed.* (Grand Rapids: Revell, 2019), 41–54.

6. Peter Wohlleben, *The Hidden Life of Trees: What They Feel, How They Communicate* (Vancouver: Greystone Books, 2016), 1–16.

CHAPTER 15. DEVELOPING A CULTURE OF GENEROSITY

1. Randy Alcorn, *The Treasure Principle: Unlocking the Secret of Joyful Giving, rev. ed.* (Colorado Springs: Multnomah, 2017), 17–32.

2. Robert Morris, *The Blessed Life: Unlocking the Rewards of Generous Living, rev. ed.* (Bloomington, MN: Bethany House, 2016), 41–58.

3. Dan Betzer, *Why Some Churches Are Blessed* (Springfield, MO: Gospel Publishing House, 2015), 22–35.

4. Randy Alcorn, *Money, Possessions, and Eternity, rev. ed.* (Carol Stream, IL: Tyndale, 2003), 145–162.

5. Roger J. Green, *The Life and Ministry of William Booth: Founder of the Salvation Army* (Nashville: Abingdon Press, 2006), 181–194.

6. Andy Stanley, *Fields of Gold: A Place Beyond Your Deepest Fears, A Prize Beyond Your Wildest Imagination* (Carol Stream, IL: Tyndale, 2004), 69–82.

CHAPTER 16. LOVING THE PLACE GOD GAVE YOU

1. Daniel Grothe, *The Power of Place: Choosing Stability in a Rootless Age* (Colorado Springs: Multnomah, 2021), 24.

2. Charles H. Kraft, quoted in Grothe, *The Power of Place*, 186.

3. Frederick Buechner, *Wishful Thinking: A Seeker's ABC, rev. ed.* (San Francisco: HarperOne, 1993), 119.

4. Grothe, *The Power of Place*, 10–11.

5. G. K. Chesterton, *Orthodoxy* (New York: Dodd, Mead and Company, 1908), 144–145.

6. Grothe, *The Power of Place*, 40.

7. Grothe, *The Power of Place*, 25.

8. Grothe, *The Power of Place*, 183–184.

CHAPTER 17. LOVING THE PEOPLE GOD SENDS

1. Molly Caldwell Crosby, *The American Plague: The Untold Story of Yellow Fever, the Epidemic That Shaped Our History* (New York: Berkley Books, 2006), 123–145.

2. Dietrich Bonhoeffer, *Life Together: The Classic Exploration of Christian Community* (New York: HarperOne, 1954), 99.

3. Bob Goff, *Everybody, Always: Becoming Love in a World Full of Setbacks and Difficult People* (Nashville: Thomas Nelson, 2018), 3.

4. Daniel Grothe, *The Power of Place: Choosing Stability in a Rootless Age* (Colorado Springs: Multnomah, 2021), 193–194.

5. Walter Lord, *The Miracle of Dunkirk* (New York: Viking Press, 1982), 174.

CHAPTER 18. GIVE ME THIS MOUNTAIN

1. James M. McPherson, *Crossroads of Freedom: Antietam* (New York: Oxford University Press, 2002), 108–122.

2. Alfred Lansing, *Endurance: Shackleton's Incredible Voyage* (New York: Basic Books, 2014), 282–291.

3. Paul R. House, *1, 2 Kings, The New American Commentary, vol. 8* (Nashville: Broadman & Holman, 1995), 284–292.

4. Warren W. Wiersbe, *Be Strong: Putting God's Power to Work in Your Life* (Colorado Springs: David C. Cook, 2010), 101–115.

5. Brian Cavanaugh, *The Sower's Seeds: One Hundred and Twenty Inspiring Stories for Preaching, Teaching, and Public Speaking*, rev. ed. (Mahwah, NJ: Paulist Press, 1989), 62–64.

Bibliography

Alcorn, Randy. The Treasure Principle: Unlocking the Secret of Joyful Giving. Rev. ed. Colorado Springs: Multnomah, 2017.

Bartleman, Frank. Azusa Street: The Roots of Modern-Day Pentecost. Plainfield, NJ: Logos International, 1980.

Batterson, Mark. The Circle Maker: Praying Circles Around Your Biggest Dreams and Greatest Fears. Grand Rapids: Zondervan, 2016.

Bernard, David K. Growing a Church. Hazelwood, MO: Word Aflame Press, 2001.

Blackaby, Henry T., and Richard Blackaby. Spiritual Leadership: Moving People on to God's Agenda. Rev. ed. Nashville: B&H Publishing Group, 2011.

Bonhoeffer, Dietrich. The Cost of Discipleship. New York: Touchstone, 1995.

Bounds, E. M. Power Through Prayer. Grand Rapids: Baker Books, 1972.

Bruce, F. F. Paul: Apostle of the Heart Set Free. Grand Rapids: Eerdmans, 2000.

Chand, Samuel R. Cracking Your Church's Culture Code: Seven Keys to Unleashing Vision and Inspiration. San Francisco: Jossey-Bass, 2011.

Chan, Francis. Letters to the Church. Colorado Springs: David C. Cook, 2018.

Coleman, Robert E. The Master Plan of Evangelism. Rev. ed. Grand Rapids: Revell, 2019.

Gleason, Stan O. Follow To Lead: The Journey of a Disciple Maker. Weldon Spring, MO: Word Aflame Press, 2016.

Greear, J. D. Gaining by Losing: Why the Future Belongs to Churches That Send. Grand Rapids: Zondervan, 2015.

Grothe, Daniel. The Power of Place: Choosing Stability in a Rootless Age. Colorado Springs: Multnomah, 2021.

Hirsch, Alan. The Forgotten Ways: Reactivating Apostolic Movements. 2nd ed. Grand Rapids: Brazos Press, 2016.

Hughes, R. Kent. Disciplines of a Godly Man. Wheaton, IL: Crossway, 2001.

Keller, Timothy. Center Church: Doing Balanced, Gospel-Centered Ministry in Your City. Grand Rapids: Zondervan, 2012.

Lloyd-Jones, D. Martyn. Studies in the Sermon on the Mount. Grand Rapids: Eerdmans, 1976.

MacDonald, Gordon. Ordering Your Private World. Rev. ed. Nashville: Thomas Nelson, 2003.

Malphurs, Aubrey. Planting Growing Churches for the 21st Century. 4th ed. Grand Rapids: Baker Books, 2011.

Maxwell, John C. The 17 Indisputable Laws of Teamwork. Nashville: Thomas Nelson, 2001.

———. The 21 Irrefutable Laws of Leadership. Rev. ed. Nashville: Thomas Nelson, 2007.

———. Everyone Communicates, Few Connect: What the Most Effective People Do Differently. Nashville: Thomas Nelson, 2010.

Morris, Robert. The Blessed Life: Unlocking the Rewards of Generous Living. Rev. ed. Bloomington, MN: Bethany House, 2019.

Nieuwhof, Carey. Didn't See It Coming: Overcoming the Seven Greatest Challenges That No One Expects and Everyone Experiences. New York: WaterBrook, 2018.

Packer, J. I. A Passion for Faithfulness: Wisdom from the Book of Nehemiah. Wheaton, IL: Crossway, 1995.

Rainer, Thom S., and Eric Geiger. Simple Church: Returning to God's Process for Making Disciples. Rev. ed. Nashville: B&H Publishing Group, 2011.

Scazzero, Peter. The Emotionally Healthy Leader. Grand Rapids: Zondervan, 2015.

Shaw, Rodney. Churchwork. Hazelwood, MO: Word Aflame Press, 2021.

Stanley, Andy. Deep and Wide: Creating Churches Unchurched People Love to Attend. 2nd ed. Grand Rapids: Zondervan, 2016.

Stetzer, Ed, and Daniel Im. Planting Missional Churches: Your Guide to Starting Churches That Multiply. 2nd ed. Nashville: B&H Academic, 2016.

Willard, Dallas. The Spirit of the Disciplines: Understanding How God Changes Lives. San Francisco: HarperSanFrancisco, 1988.

Wright, Christopher J. H. The Mission of God: Unlocking the Bible's Grand Narrative. Downers Grove, IL: IVP Academic, 2006.

Recommended Resources

The following resources have been especially helpful in church planting, discipleship, and leadership development. While no book can replace the leading of the Spirit or the authority of Scripture, these works provide practical insight and encouragement for those committed to building the Kingdom.

CHURCH PLANTING

A Life so Lovely: Encouragement for the Church Planter's Wife — Anna Ruth Frazier

A meaningful and encouraging resource for the church planter's wife, addressing the unique challenges and calling of ministry life with grace and wisdom.

DISCIPLESHIP

Follow to Lead: The Journey of a Disciple Maker — Stan O. Gleason

A clear and Apostolic approach to discipleship that emphasizes developing believers into leaders who reproduce others.

This Book Is for You: Everyone a Disciple Maker — Chad Erickson

A practical and accessible call for every believer to engage in disciple-making, with simple steps that can be implemented immediately.

LEADERSHIP

Churchwork — Rodney Shaw

A foundational Apostolic resource focused on the practical work of building and sustaining a local church.

Growing a Church — David K. Bernard

A balanced approach to church growth that integrates spiritual principles, structure, and leadership development.

The Leadership Gameplan: Develop Unstoppable Leaders — Evan Grizzle

A strategic guide to developing strong, effective leaders who can carry vision and sustain momentum in ministry.

FINAL ENCOURAGEMENT

Learn from those who have gone before you, but never lose sight of the voice of God in your own calling. These resources can sharpen your thinking and strengthen your approach—but ultimately, it is the Spirit of God working through yielded vessels that builds His Church.

Acknowledgements

This book is the result of a lifetime spent surrounded by incredible leaders who have shaped my life, my thinking, and my leadership. I am deeply grateful for the influence of so many people who have poured into me along the way.

I am especially thankful for the church planters I have had the privilege to serve alongside, the Metro Missionaries I was honored to support during my time as Metro Missions Coordinator, and the current Missions America church planters I now serve as Missions America Director. Each of you has left a lasting mark on my life and ministry.

FAMILY

To my parents, Joe and Barbara Smith—thank you for your unwavering love, sacrifice, and example. To my brother, Gary Smith, and to my in-laws, Danny and Demetris Davis, thank you for your support and encouragement. I am also grateful for my grandparents, Robert and Lawana Burchyett, and for the extended blessing of aunts, uncles, brothers- and sisters-in-law, cousins, nieces, and nephews. Your love has been a constant foundation in my life.

FRIENDS

Nathan and Victoria Batson, Tim and Lois Greene, Karen Harding, Bill and Shawna Hobson, Aubrey & Donna Jayroe, Stephen & Erma Judd, Jimmy & Jelaine Lumpkin, Tim & Julie Zuniga; your friendship has been a gift. Thank you for your loyalty, your encouragement, and your presence.

PASTORS

I am indebted to the pastors who have spoken into my life and ministry: Don Johnson, Bob McCool Sr., Bob Burchyett, E. D. Puckett, Jimmy Brindley, Ray Romain, Bobby McCool Jr., D. D. Davis, and Doug Davis. Your leadership and influence have helped shape who I am today.

CHURCH PLANTING LEADERS

Thank you to the leaders who have invested in the work of church planting and in my life personally: Jack Cunningham, Carlton Coon, Jimmy Toney, Scott Sistrunk, Bill Hobson, Scott Armstrong, Buddy Buie, Brian Kinsey, Andy Smith, and David Wiseman.

THE ASSEMBLIES OF THE LORD JESUS CHRIST EXECUTIVE BOARD

I am grateful for the leadership and vision of Kenneth Carpenter, Jonathan Vazquez, Kenneth Allen, Robert Wimberley, and Joshua Wilson. Thank you for your commitment to advancing the Kingdom.

THE MISSIONS AMERICA EXECUTIVE COMMITTEE

Evan Grizzle, Alex Fallin, Brandon Frazier, Dan Mundy, Rob Jones, James Archambeault, Chad Erickson, Joseph Perez, Tim Gill, Mark McCool, and David Poole—thank you for your partnership, your passion, and your commitment to seeing churches planted across this nation.

PRAYER PARTNERS

Caleb Flowers, Julie Garner, Paul Grady, Kerri Haley, Dylan Moody, Cindy Nooner, Shari Shelton, and Ginger Smith, thank you for standing in the gap through prayer. Your faithfulness in intercession has strengthened me in ways words cannot fully express. This work is not accomplished by effort alone, but by the power of God, and your prayers have made a lasting difference.

FINAL WORD

To every church planter laboring in the harvest—this book is for you. Your calling matters. Your sacrifice matters. And the work you are doing is making an eternal difference.

About the Author

Steve Smith pastors Faith Apostolic Church in Memphis, Tennessee, where he serves as the first pastor. He and his family also pioneered Westchester Apostolic Church in White Plains, New York, helping establish a strong Apostolic witness in the New York City metro area.

He currently serves as the Missions America Director for the Assemblies of the Lord Jesus Christ (ALJC), where he leads national initiatives focused on church planting and evangelism across the United States. In this role, he works closely with church planters, districts, and leaders to equip and support the planting of new churches in communities across the nation.

Previously, he served as the Metro Missions Coordinator for the North American Missions Division of the United Pentecostal Church, International (UPCI), where he helped develop and strengthen church planting efforts in metropolitan areas.

He is passionate about raising up leaders, equipping church planters, and helping local churches reach their communities with the gospel of Jesus Christ. His ministry reflects a deep commitment to Apostolic doctrine, discipleship, and the multiplication of healthy, Spirit-filled churches.

He and his wife, Lorrie, are blessed with three sons—Landry, Clancy, and Colyer.

Take the Next Step

The work of church planting is not reserved for a select few, it is the responsibility of the Church. Across the United States, there are cities, communities, and neighborhoods that are waiting for a Spirit-filled, Apostolic witness. The harvest is ready, and the call is clear.

The question is not whether something needs to be done. The question is, what is your next step?

SUPPORT THE MISSION

Missions America exists to help plant and strengthen Apostolic churches across this nation. Through your financial support, you can play a direct role in reaching cities, equipping church planters, and advancing the gospel into places that need it most.

Your giving makes a difference. Every seed sown helps send laborers into the harvest.

ANSWER THE CALL

If you feel the stirring to plant a church, do not ignore it. God is still calling men and women to step out in faith and establish new works.

Missions America is committed to walking with you through that journey, providing guidance, support, and a pathway forward as you pursue the call of God on your life.

GROW AND BE EQUIPPED

Healthy church planting requires intentional preparation. Whether you are just beginning to explore the call or already taking steps toward planting, training is essential.

Propel is a three-session church planter training experience offered at the district level, designed to help you recognize your calling, prepare for the work, and take your next step with confidence.

Forward is an online leadership development platform that provides ongoing equipping through podcasts and e-courses, helping you grow as a leader and strengthen your ministry over time.

GET CONNECTED

To learn more about how you can support, plant, or be trained, visit:

https://missionsamerica.aljc.org/

A FINAL WORD

God is still building His Church. The opportunity to be part of that work is one of the greatest privileges you will ever be given.

Take the next step.

www.ingramcontent.com/pod-product-compliance
Lightning Source LLC
Chambersburg PA
CBHW020337180726
47991CB00020B/1743